NLN PAX Practice

Practice Test Questions for the PAX-RN

We strongly recommend that students check with exam providers for up-to-date information regarding test content.

Please note that PAX RN is administered by the National League of Nursing which was not involved in the production of, and does not endorse, this product.

ISBN-13: 9781772453270

Version 8 December 2020

About Complete Test Preparation Inc.

The Complete Test Preparation Team has been publishing high quality study materials since 2005. Over one million students visit our websites every year, and thousands of students, teachers and parents all over the world (over 100 countries) have purchased our teaching materials, curriculum, study guides and practice tests.

Complete Test Preparation Inc. is committed to providing students with the best study materials and practice tests available on the market. Members of our team combine years of teaching experience, with experienced writers and editors, all with advanced degrees.

Published by
Complete Test Preparation Inc.
Victoria BC Canada

Visit us on the web at https://www.test-preparation.ca
Printed in the USA

Feedback

We welcome your feedback. Email us at feedback@test-preparation.ca with your comments and suggestions. We carefully review all suggestions and often incorporate reader suggestions into upcoming versions. As a Print on Demand Publisher, we update our products frequently.

https://www.facebook.com/CompleteTestPreparation/

https://www.youtube.com/user/MrTestPreparation

https://www.instagram.com/test.preparation/

Contents

Getting Started

Congratulations! By deciding to take the Registered Nursing Program (PAX RN) Exam, you have taken the first step toward a great future! Of course, there is no point in taking this important examination unless you intend to do your best to earn the highest grade you possibly can. That means getting yourself organized and discovering the best approaches, methods and strategies to master the material. Yes, that will require real effort and dedication, but if you are willing to focus your energy and devote the study time necessary, before you know it you will be opening that letter of acceptance to the school of your dreams.

We know that taking on a new endeavour can be scary, and it is easy to feel unsure of where to begin. That's where we come in. This study guide is designed to help you improve your test-taking skills, show you a few tricks of the trade and increase both your competency and confidence.

The Registered Nursing Program PAX RN Exam

The PAX RN Modules are: Mathematics, Verbal Ability (Reading Comprehension and Vocabulary), and Science which includes, Biology, Chemistry, Physics, Basic Scientific principals and Earth Science.

While we seek to make our guide as comprehensive as possible, note that like all entrance exams, the PAX RN Exam might be adjusted at some future point. New material might be added, or content that is no longer relevant or applicable might be removed. It is always a good idea to give the materials you receive when you register to take the PAX RN a careful review.

The PAX RN Study Plan

Now that you have made the decision to take the PAX RN, it is time to get started. Before you do another thing, you will need to figure out a plan of attack. The very best study tip is to start early! The longer the time period you devote to regular study practice, the more likely you will be to retain the material and access it quickly. If you thought that 1x20 is the same as 2x10, guess what? It really is not, when it comes to study time. Reviewing material for just an hour per day over the course of 20 days is far better than studying for two hours a day for only 10 days. The more often you revisit a particular piece of information, the better you will know it. Not only will your grasp and understanding be better, but your ability to reach into your brain and quickly and efficiently pull out the tidbit you need, will be greatly enhanced as well.

The great Chinese scholar and philosopher Confucius believed that true knowledge could be defined as knowing what you know and what you do not know. The first step in preparing for the PAX RN Exam is to assess your strengths and weaknesses. You may already have an idea of what you know and what you do not know, but evaluating yourself using our Self- Assessment modules for each of the three areas, Math, Science and Verbal Ability, will clarify the details.

Making a Study Schedule

To make your study time the most productive, you will need to develop a study plan. The purpose of the plan is to organize all the bits of pieces of information in such a way that you will not feel overwhelmed. Rome was not built in a day, and learning everything you will need to know to pass the PAX RN Exam is going to take time, too. Arranging the material you need to learn into manageable chunks is the best way to go. Each study session should make you feel as though you have accomplished your goal, or at least are closer, and your goal is simply to learn what you planned to learn during that particular session. Try to organize the content in such a way that each study session builds on previous ones. That way, you will retain the information, be better able to access it, and review the previous bits and pieces at the same time.

Self-assessment

The Best Study Tip! The very best study tip is to start early! The longer you study regularly, the more you will retain and 'learn' the material. Studying for 1 hour per day for 20 days is far better than studying for 2 hours for 10 days.

What don't you know?

The first step is to assess your strengths and weaknesses. You may already have an idea of where your weaknesses are, or you can take our Self-assessment modules for each of the areas, Math, Science and Verbal Ability.

Exam Component	Rate 1 to 5
Verbal Ability	
Paragraph & Passage Comprehension	
Vocabulary	
Math Fractions, Decimals, Percent	
Word Problems	
Percent	
Median and Mode	
Scientific Notation	
Quadratics and Polynomials	
Speed and Momentum	
Basic Algebra	

Science	
Biology	
Physics	
Earth Science	
Chemistry	

Making a Study Schedule

The key to making a study plan is to divide the material you need to learn into manageable size and learn it, while at the same time reviewing the material that you already know.

Using the table above, any scores of 3 or below, you need to spend time learning, reviewing and practicing this subject area. A score of 4 means you need to review the material, but you don't have to spend time re-learning. A score of 5 and you are OK with just an occasional review before the exam.

A score of 0 or 1 means you really need to work on this area and should allocate the most time and the highest priority. Some students prefer a 5-day plan and others a 10-day plan. It also depends on how much time until the exam.

Here is an example of a 5-day plan based on an example from the table above:

Fractions: 1 Study 1 hour everyday – review on last day
Biology: 3 Study 1 hour for 2 days then ½ hour a day, then review
Vocabulary: 4 Review every second day
Word Problems: 2 Study 1 hour on the first day – then ½ hour everyday
Reading Comprehension: 5 Review for ½ hour every other day
Algebra: 5 Review for ½ hour every other day
Chemistry: 5 very confident – review a few times.

Based on this, here is a sample study plan:

Day	**Subject**	**Time**
Monday		
Study	Fractions	1 hour
Study	Word Problems	1 hour
	½ hour break	
Study	Biology	1 hour
Review	Chemistry	½ hour
Tuesday		
Study	Fractions	1 hour
Study	Word Problems	½ hour
	½ hour break	
Study	Decimals	½ hour
Review	Vocabulary	½ hour
Review	Grammar	½ hour
Wednesday		
Study	Fractions	1 hour
Study	Word Problems	½ hour
	½ hour break	
Study	Biology	½ hour
Review	Chemistry	½ hour
Thursday		
Study	Fractions	½ hour
Study	Word Problems	½ hour
Review	Biology	½ hour
	½ hour break	
Review	Grammar	½ hour
Review	Vocabulary	½ hour

Friday		
Review	Fractions	½ hour
Review	Word Problems	½ hour
Review	Biology	½ hour
	½ hour break	
Review	Vocabulary	½ hour
Review	Grammar	½ hour

Practice Test Questions Set 1

The questions below are not the same as you will find on the PAX RN - that would be too easy! And nobody knows what the questions will be and they change all the time. Below are general questions that cover the same subject areas as the PAX RN. So the format and exact wording of the questions may differ slightly, and change from year to year, if you can answer the questions below, you will have no problem with the PAX RN.

For the best results, take this Practice Test as if it were the real exam. Set aside time when you will not be disturbed, and a location that is quiet and free of distractions. Read the instructions carefully, read each question carefully, and answer to the best of your ability.

Use the bubble answer sheets provided. When you have completed the Practice Test, check your answer against the Answer Key and read the explanation provided.

Do not attempt more than one set of practice test questions in one day. After completing the first practice test, wait two or three days before attempting the second set of questions.

Section I – Verbal Ability
Questions: 80 **Time:** 60 Minutes

Section II – Mathematics
Questions: 50 **Time:** 60 Minutes

Section III – Science
Questions: 75 **Time:** 60 minutes

Answer Sheet – Verbal Ability

1. (A) (B) (C) (D)	21. (A) (B) (C) (D)	41. (A) (B) (C) (D)	61. (A) (B) (C) (D)
2. (A) (B) (C) (D)	22. (A) (B) (C) (D)	42. (A) (B) (C) (D)	62. (A) (B) (C) (D)
3. (A) (B) (C) (D)	23. (A) (B) (C) (D)	43. (A) (B) (C) (D)	63. (A) (B) (C) (D)
4. (A) (B) (C) (D)	24. (A) (B) (C) (D)	44. (A) (B) (C) (D)	64. (A) (B) (C) (D)
5. (A) (B) (C) (D)	25. (A) (B) (C) (D)	45. (A) (B) (C) (D)	65. (A) (B) (C) (D)
6. (A) (B) (C) (D)	26. (A) (B) (C) (D)	46. (A) (B) (C) (D)	66. (A) (B) (C) (D)
7. (A) (B) (C) (D)	27. (A) (B) (C) (D)	47. (A) (B) (C) (D)	67. (A) (B) (C) (D)
8. (A) (B) (C) (D)	28. (A) (B) (C) (D)	48. (A) (B) (C) (D)	68. (A) (B) (C) (D)
9. (A) (B) (C) (D)	29. (A) (B) (C) (D)	49. (A) (B) (C) (D)	69. (A) (B) (C) (D)
10. (A) (B) (C) (D)	30. (A) (B) (C) (D)	50. (A) (B) (C) (D)	70. (A) (B) (C) (D)
11. (A) (B) (C) (D)	31. (A) (B) (C) (D)	51. (A) (B) (C) (D)	71. (A) (B) (C) (D)
12. (A) (B) (C) (D)	32. (A) (B) (C) (D)	52. (A) (B) (C) (D)	72. (A) (B) (C) (D)
13. (A) (B) (C) (D)	33. (A) (B) (C) (D)	53. (A) (B) (C) (D)	73. (A) (B) (C) (D)
14. (A) (B) (C) (D)	34. (A) (B) (C) (D)	54. (A) (B) (C) (D)	74. (A) (B) (C) (D)
15. (A) (B) (C) (D)	35. (A) (B) (C) (D)	55. (A) (B) (C) (D)	75. (A) (B) (C) (D)
16. (A) (B) (C) (D)	36. (A) (B) (C) (D)	56. (A) (B) (C) (D)	76. (A) (B) (C) (D)
17. (A) (B) (C) (D)	37. (A) (B) (C) (D)	57. (A) (B) (C) (D)	77. (A) (B) (C) (D)
18. (A) (B) (C) (D)	38. (A) (B) (C) (D)	58. (A) (B) (C) (D)	78. (A) (B) (C) (D)
19. (A) (B) (C) (D)	39. (A) (B) (C) (D)	59. (A) (B) (C) (D)	79. (A) (B) (C) (D)
20. (A) (B) (C) (D)	40. (A) (B) (C) (D)	60. (A) (B) (C) (D)	80. (A) (B) (C) (D)

Answer Sheet – Mathematics

1. (A) (B) (C) (D)
2. (A) (B) (C) (D)
3. (A) (B) (C) (D)
4. (A) (B) (C) (D)
5. (A) (B) (C) (D)
6. (A) (B) (C) (D)
7. (A) (B) (C) (D)
8. (A) (B) (C) (D)
9. (A) (B) (C) (D)
10. (A) (B) (C) (D)
11. (A) (B) (C) (D)
12. (A) (B) (C) (D)
13. (A) (B) (C) (D)
14. (A) (B) (C) (D)
15. (A) (B) (C) (D)
16. (A) (B) (C) (D)
17. (A) (B) (C) (D)
18. (A) (B) (C) (D)
19. (A) (B) (C) (D)
20. (A) (B) (C) (D)
21. (A) (B) (C) (D)
22. (A) (B) (C) (D)
23. (A) (B) (C) (D)
24. (A) (B) (C) (D)
25. (A) (B) (C) (D)
26. (A) (B) (C) (D)
27. (A) (B) (C) (D)
28. (A) (B) (C) (D)
29. (A) (B) (C) (D)
30. (A) (B) (C) (D)
31. (A) (B) (C) (D)
32. (A) (B) (C) (D)
33. (A) (B) (C) (D)
34. (A) (B) (C) (D)
35. (A) (B) (C) (D)
36. (A) (B) (C) (D)
37. (A) (B) (C) (D)
38. (A) (B) (C) (D)
39. (A) (B) (C) (D)
40. (A) (B) (C) (D)
41. (A) (B) (C) (D)
42. (A) (B) (C) (D)
43. (A) (B) (C) (D)
44. (A) (B) (C) (D)
45. (A) (B) (C) (D)
46. (A) (B) (C) (D)
47. (A) (B) (C) (D)
48. (A) (B) (C) (D)
49. (A) (B) (C) (D)
50. (A) (B) (C) (D)

Answer Sheet – Science

1. (A) (B) (C) (D)
2. (A) (B) (C) (D)
3. (A) (B) (C) (D)
4. (A) (B) (C) (D)
5. (A) (B) (C) (D)
6. (A) (B) (C) (D)
7. (A) (B) (C) (D)
8. (A) (B) (C) (D)
9. (A) (B) (C) (D)
10. (A) (B) (C) (D)
11. (A) (B) (C) (D)
12. (A) (B) (C) (D)
13. (A) (B) (C) (D)
14. (A) (B) (C) (D)
15. (A) (B) (C) (D)
16. (A) (B) (C) (D)
17. (A) (B) (C) (D)
18. (A) (B) (C) (D)
19. (A) (B) (C) (D)
20. (A) (B) (C) (D)
21. (A) (B) (C) (D)
22. (A) (B) (C) (D)
23. (A) (B) (C) (D)
24. (A) (B) (C) (D)
25. (A) (B) (C) (D)
26. (A) (B) (C) (D)
27. (A) (B) (C) (D)
28. (A) (B) (C) (D)
29. (A) (B) (C) (D)
30. (A) (B) (C) (D)
31. (A) (B) (C) (D)
32. (A) (B) (C) (D)
33. (A) (B) (C) (D)
34. (A) (B) (C) (D)
35. (A) (B) (C) (D)
36. (A) (B) (C) (D)
37. (A) (B) (C) (D)
38. (A) (B) (C) (D)
39. (A) (B) (C) (D)
40. (A) (B) (C) (D)
41. (A) (B) (C) (D)
42. (A) (B) (C) (D)
43. (A) (B) (C) (D)
44. (A) (B) (C) (D)
45. (A) (B) (C) (D)
46. (A) (B) (C) (D)
47. (A) (B) (C) (D)
48. (A) (B) (C) (D)
49. (A) (B) (C) (D)
50. (A) (B) (C) (D)
51. (A) (B) (C) (D)
52. (A) (B) (C) (D)
53. (A) (B) (C) (D)
54. (A) (B) (C) (D)
55. (A) (B) (C) (D)
56. (A) (B) (C) (D)
57. (A) (B) (C) (D)
58. (A) (B) (C) (D)
59. (A) (B) (C) (D)
60. (A) (B) (C) (D)
61. (A) (B) (C) (D)
62. (A) (B) (C) (D)
63. (A) (B) (C) (D)
64. (A) (B) (C) (D)
65. (A) (B) (C) (D)
66. (A) (B) (C) (D)
67. (A) (B) (C) (D)
68. (A) (B) (C) (D)
69. (A) (B) (C) (D)
70. (A) (B) (C) (D)
71. (A) (B) (C) (D)
72. (A) (B) (C) (D)
73. (A) (B) (C) (D)
74. (A) (B) (C) (D)
75. (A) (B) (C) (D)

Section I - Verbal Ability

Directions: The following questions are based on several reading passages. Each passage is followed by a series of questions. Read each passage carefully, and then answer the questions based on it. You may reread the passage as often as you wish. When you have finished answering the questions based on one passage, go right onto the next passage. Choose the best answer based on the information given and implied.

Questions 1 – 4 refer to the following passage.

Passage 1 - The Life of Helen Keller

Many people have heard of Helen Keller. She is famous because she was unable to see or hear, but learned to speak and read and went onto attend college and earn a degree. Her life is a very interesting story, one that she developed into an autobiography, which was then adapted into both a stage play and a movie. How did Helen Keller overcome her disabilities to become a famous woman? Read on to find out. Helen Keller was not born blind and deaf. When she was a small baby, she had a very high fever for several days. As a result of her sudden illness, baby Helen lost her eyesight and her hearing. Because she was so young when she went deaf and blind, Helen Keller never had any recollection of being able to see or hear. Since she could not hear, she could not learn to talk. Since she could not see, it was difficult for her to move around. For the first six years of her life, her world was very still and dark.

Imagine what Helen's childhood was like. She could not hear her mother's voice. She could not see the beauty of her parent's farm. She could not recognize who was giving her a hug, or a bath or even where her bedroom was each night. Worse, she could not communicate with her parents in any way. She could not express her feelings or tell them the things she wanted. It must have been a very sad childhood.

When Helen was six years old, her parents hired her a teacher named Anne Sullivan. Anne was a young woman who was almost blind. However, she could hear and she could read Braille, so she was a perfect teacher for young Helen. At first, Anne had a very hard time teaching Helen anything. She described her first impression of Helen as a "wild thing, not a child." Helen did not like Anne at first either. She bit and hit Anne when Anne tried to teach her. However, the two of them eventually came to have a great deal of love and respect.

Anne taught Helen to hear by putting her hands on people's throats. She could feel the sounds people made. In time, Helen learned to feel what people said. Next, Anne taught Helen to read Braille, which is a way that books are written for the blind. Finally, Anne taught Helen to talk. Although Helen did learn to talk, it was hard for anyone but Anne to understand her.

As Helen grew older, she amazed more and more people with her story. She went to college and wrote books about her life. She gave talks to the public, with Anne at her side, translating her words. Today, both Anne Sullivan and Helen Keller are famous women who are respected for their lives' work.

1. Helen Keller could not see and hear and so, what was her biggest problem in childhood?

a. Inability to communicate

b. Inability to walk

c. Inability to play

d. Inability to eat

2. Helen learned to hear by feeling the vibrations people made when they spoke. What were these vibrations were felt through?

a. Mouth

b. Throat

c. Ears

d. Lips

3. From the passage, we can infer that Anne Sullivan was a patient teacher. We can infer this because

a. Helen hit and bit her and Anne remained her teacher.

b. Anne taught Helen to read only.

c. Anne was hard of hearing too.

d. Anne wanted to be a teacher.

4. Helen Keller learned to speak but Anne translated her words when she spoke in public. The reason Helen needed a translator was because

a. Helen spoke another language.

b. Helen's words were hard for people to understand.

c. Helen spoke very quietly.

d. Helen did not speak but only used sign language.

Questions 5 – 7 refer to the following passage.

Passage 2 - Ways Characters Communicate in Theater

Playwrights give their characters voices in a way that gives depth and added meaning to what happens on stage during their play. There are different types of speech in scripts that allow characters to talk with themselves, with other characters, and even with the audience.

It is very unique to theater that characters may talk "to themselves." When characters do this, the speech they give is called a soliloquy. Soliloquies are usually poetic, introspective, moving, and can tell audience members about the feelings, motivations, or suspicions of an individual character without that character having to reveal them to other characters on stage. "To be or not to be" is a famous soliloquy given by Hamlet as he considers difficult but important themes, such as life and death.

The most common type of communication in plays is when one character is speaking to another or a group of other characters. This is generally called dialogue, but can also be called monologue if one character speaks without being interrupted for a long time. It is not necessarily the most important type of communication, but it is the most common because the plot of the play cannot really progress without it.
Lastly, and most unique to theater (although it has been used somewhat in film) is when a character speaks directly to the audience. This is called an aside, and scripts usually specifically direct actors to do this. Asides are usually comical, an inside joke between the character and the audience, and very short. The actor will usually face the audience when delivering them, even if it's for a moment, so the audience can recognize this move as an aside.

All three of these types of communication are important to the art of theater, and have been perfected by famous playwrights like Shakespeare. Understanding these types of communication can help an audience member grasp what is artful about the script and action of a play.

5. According to the passage, characters in plays communicate to

a. move the plot forward

b. show the private thoughts and feelings of one character

c. make the audience laugh

d. add beauty and artistry to the play

6. When Hamlet delivers "To be or not to be," he can be described as

a. solitary

b. thoughtful

c. dramatic

d. hopeless

7. The author uses parentheses to punctuate "although it has been used somewhat in film,"

a. to show that films are less important

b. instead of using commas so that the sentence is not interrupted

c. because parenthesis help separate details that are not as important

d. to show that films are not as artistic

Questions 8 – 10 refer to the following passage.

Passage 3 - Low Blood Sugar

As the name suggest, low blood sugar is low sugar levels in the bloodstream. This can occur when you have not eaten properly and undertake strenuous activity, or, when you are very hungry. When Low blood sugar occurs regularly and is ongoing, it is a medical condition called hypoglycemia. This condition can occur in diabetics and in healthy adults.

Causes of low blood sugar can include excessive alcohol consumption, metabolic problems, stomach surgery, pancreas, liver or kidneys problems, as well as a side-effect of some medications.

Symptoms

There are different symptoms depending on the severity of the case.

Mild hypoglycemia can lead to feelings of nausea and hunger. The patient may also feel nervous, jittery and have fast heart beats. Sweaty skin, clammy and cold skin are likely symptoms.
Moderate hypoglycemia can result in a short temper, confusion, nervousness, fear and blurring of vision. The patient may feel weak and unsteady.

Severe cases of hypoglycemia can lead to seizures, coma,

fainting spells, nightmares, headaches, excessive sweats and severe tiredness.

Diagnosis of low blood sugar

A doctor can diagnosis this medical condition by asking the patient questions and testing blood and urine samples. Home testing kits are available for patients to monitor blood sugar levels. It is important to see a qualified doctor though. The doctor can administer tests to ensure that will safely rule out other medical conditions that could affect blood sugar levels.

Treatment

Quick treatments include drinking or eating foods and drinks with high sugar contents. Good examples include soda, fruit juice, hard candy and raisins. Glucose energy tablets can also help. Doctors may also recommend medications and well as changes in diet and exercise routine to treat chronic low blood sugar.

8. Based on the article, which of the following is true?

a. Low blood sugar can happen to anyone.

b. Low blood sugar only happens to diabetics.

c. Low blood sugar can occur even.

d. None of the statements are true.

9. Which of the following are the author's opinion?

a. Quick treatments include drinking or eating foods and drinks with high sugar contents.

b. None of the statements are opinions.

c. This condition can occur in diabetics and in healthy adults.

d. There are different symptoms depending on the severity of the case

10. What is the author's purpose?

a. To inform

b. To persuade

c. To entertain

d. To analyse

11. Which of the following is not a detail?

a. A doctor can diagnosis this medical condition by asking the patient questions and testing.

b. A doctor will test blood and urine samples.

c. Glucose energy tablets can also help.

d. Home test kits monitor blood sugar levels.

d. None of the above.

Questions 12 – 15 refer to the following passage.

How To Get A Good Nights Sleep

Sleep is just as essential for healthy living as water, air and food. Sleep allows the body to rest and replenish depleted energy levels. Sometimes we may for various reasons have trouble sleeping which has a serious effect on our health. Those who have prolonged sleeping problems are facing a serious medical condition and should see a qualified doctor when possible for help. Here is simple guide that can help you sleep better at night.
Try to create a natural pattern of waking up and sleeping around the same time every day. This means avoiding going to bed too early and oversleeping past your usual wake up time. Going to bed and getting up at radically different times everyday confuses your body clock. Try to establish a natural rhythm as much as you can.

Exercises and a bit of physical activity can help you sleep better at night. If you are having problem sleeping, try to be as active as you can during the day. If you are tired from physical activity, falling asleep is a natural and easy process for your body. If you remain inactive during the day, you will find it harder to sleep properly at night. Try walking, jogging, swimming or simple stretches as you get close to your bed time.

Afternoon naps are great to refresh you during the day, but they may also keep you awake at night. If you feel sleepy during the day, get up, take a walk and get busy to keep from sleeping. Stretching is a good way to increase blood flow to the brain and keep you alert so that you don't sleep during the day. This will help you sleep better night.

> A warm bath or a glass of milk in the evening can help your body relax and prepare for sleep. A cold bath will wake you up and keep you up for several hours. Also avoid eating too late before bed.

12. How would you describe this sentence?

a. A recommendation

b. An opinion

c. A fact

d. A diagnosis

13. Which of the following is an alternative title for this article?

a. Exercise and a good night's sleep

b. Benefits of a good night's sleep

c. Tips for a good night's sleep

d. Lack of sleep is a serious medical condition

14. Which of the following cannot be inferred from this article?

a. Biking is helpful for getting a good night's sleep
b. Mental activity is helpful for getting a good night's sleep
c. Eating bedtime snacks is not recommended
d. Getting up at the same time is helpful for a good night's sleep

15. What is a disadvantage of taking naps?

a. They may keep you awake.
b. There are no disadvantages
c. They may help you sleep better
d. They may affect your diet

Question 16 refers to the following Table of Contents.

Contents

Science Self-assessment 81
Answer Key 91
Science Tutorials 96
Scientific Method 96
Biology 99
Heredity: Genes and Mutation 104
Classification 108
Ecology 110
Chemistry 112
Energy: Kinetic and Mechanical 126
Energy: Work and Power 130
Force: Newton's Three Laws 132

16. Consider the table of contents above. What page would you find information about natural selection and adaptation?

a. 81
b. 90
c. 110
d. 132

Questions 17 – 19 refer to the following passage.

Passage 5 - Pearl Harbor

A Day That Will Live in Infamy! Attack on Pearl Harbor
In 1941, the world was at war. The United States was trying to stay out of the conflict. In Europe, the countries of Germany and Italy had formed an alliance to expand their land and territory. Germany had already taken over Poland, Denmark, and parts of France. They were heading next toward England and due to all the fighting in Europe, there were battles taking place as far south as North Africa, where the German and Italian armies were fighting the British.

This got even worse when the Asian nation of Japan formed an alliance with Germany and Italy. Together, the three countries called themselves, the AXIS. Now, the war was in the Pacific as well as in Europe and Northern Africa. Many Americans felt that perhaps now was the time for the United States to join with its ally, Great Britain and stop the Axis from taking over more regions of the world.

In 1941, Franklin Roosevelt was President of the United States. His fear at the time was that Japan would try to take over many countries in Asia. He did not want to see that happen, so he moved some of the United States warships that had been stationed in San Diego, to the military base at Pearl Harbor, in Honolulu, Hawaii.

Japan quietly plotted their attack. They waited until the early hours of the morning on Sunday, December 7, 1941. Then, 350 Japanese war plans began to drop bombs on the U.S. ships at Pearl Harbor. The first bombs fell at 7:48 am and a mere 90 minutes later, the attack was over. Pearl Harbor was decimated. 8 battleships were damaged. Eleven ships were sunk and 300 U.S. planes were destroyed. Most devastating was the loss of life 2,400 U.S. military members was killed in the attack and 1, 282 were injured.

President Roosevelt addressed the country via the radio and said "Today is a day that will live in infamy." He asked Congress to declare war on Japan. War was declared on Japan on December 8th and on Germany and Italy on December 11th. The United States had entered World War Two.

17. After reading the passage, what can we infer infamy means?

a. Famous

b. Remembered in a good way

c. Remembered in a bad way

d. Easily forgotten

18. What three countries formed the Axis?

a. Italy, England, Germany

b. United States, England, Italy

c. Germany, Japan, Italy

d. Germany, Japan, United States

19. What do you think was President Roosevelt's reason for moving warships to Pearl Harbor?

a. He feared Japan would bomb San Diego

b. He knew Japan was going to attack Pearl Harbor

c. He was planning to attack Japan

d. He wanted to try to protect Asian countries from Japanese takeover

20. Why do you think Japan chose a Sunday morning at 7:48 am for their attack?

a. They knew the military slept late

b. There is a law against bombing countries on a Sunday

c. They wanted the attack to catch people by surprise

d. That was the only free time they had to attack.

Questions 21 - 24 refer to the following recipe.

If You Have Allergies, You're Not Alone

People who experience allergies might joke that their immune systems have let them down or are seriously lacking. Truthfully though, people who experience allergic reactions or allergy symptoms during certain times of the year have heightened immune systems that are, "better" than those of people who have perfectly healthy but less militant immune systems.

Still, when a person has an allergic reaction, they are having an adverse reaction to a substance that is considered normal to most people. Mild allergic reactions usually have symptoms like itching, runny nose, red eyes, or bumps or discoloration of the skin. More serious allergic reactions, such as those to animal and insect poisons or certain foods, may result in the closing of the throat, swelling of the eyes, low blood pressure, inability to breath, and can even be fatal.

Different treatments help different allergies, and which one a person uses depends on the nature and severity of the allergy. It is recommended to patients with severe allergies to take extra precautions, such as carrying an EpiPen, which treats anaphylactic shock and may prevent death, always in order for the remedy to be readily available and more effective. When an allergy is not so severe, treatments may be used just relieve a person of uncomfortable symptoms. Over the counter allergy medicines treat milder symptoms, and can be bought at any grocery store and used in moderation to help people with allergies live normally.

There are many tests available to assess whether a person has allergies or what they may be allergic to, and advances in these tests and the medicine used to treat patients continues to improve. Despite this fact, allergies still affect many people throughout the year or even every day. Medicines used to treat allergies have side-effects, and it is difficult to bring the body into balance with the use of medicine. Regardless, many of those who live with allergies are grateful for what is available and find it useful in maintaining their lifestyles.

21. According to this passage, which group does the word "militant" belong in

a. sickly, ailing, faint

b. strength, power, vigor

c. active, fighting, warring

d. worn, tired, breaking down

22. The author says that "medicines used to treat allergies have side-effects of their own" to

a. point out that doctors aren't very good at diagnosing and treating allergies

b. argue that because of the large number of people with allergies, a cure will never be found

c. explain that allergy medicines aren't cures and some compromise must be made

d. argue that more wholesome remedies should be researched and medicines banned

23. It can be inferred that _______ recommend that some people with allergies carry medicine with them.

a. the author

b. doctors

c. the makers of EpiPen

d. people with allergies

24. The author has written this passage to

a. inform readers on symptoms of allergies so people with allergies can get help

b. persuade readers to be proud of having allergies

c. inform readers on different remedies so people with allergies receive the right help

d. describe different types of allergies, their symptoms, and their remedies

Questions 25 - 26 refer to the following email.

SUBJECT: MEDICAL STAFF CHANGES

To all staff:

This email is to advise you of a paper on recommended medical staff changes has been posted to the Human Resources website.

The contents are of primary interest to medical staff, other staff may be interested in reading it, particularly those in medical support roles.

The paper deals with several major issues:

1. Improving our ability to attract top quality staff to the hospital, and retain our existing staff. These changes will make our position and departmental names internationally recognizable and comparable with North American and North Asian departments and positions.

2. Improving our ability to attract top quality staff by introducing greater flexibility in the departmental structure.

3. General comments on issues to be further discussed relative to research staff.

The changes outlined in this paper are significant. I encourage you to read the document and send to me any comments you may have, so that it can be enhanced and improved.

Gordon Simms
Administrator,
Seven Oaks Regional Hospital

25. Are all hospital staff required to read the document posted to the
Human Resources website?

a. Yes all staff are required to read the document.

b. No, reading the document is optional.

c. Only medical staff are required to read the document.

d. none of the above are correct.

26. Have the changes to medical staff been made?

a. Yes, the changes have been made.

b. No, the changes are only being discussed.

c. Some of the changes have been made.

d. None of the choices are correct.

Questions 27 – 30 refer to the following passage.

When a Poet Longs to Mourn, He Writes an Elegy

Poems are an expressive, especially emotional, form of writing. They have been in literature virtually from the time civilizations invented the written word. Poets often portrayed as moody, secluded, and even troubled, but this is because poets are introspective and feel deeply about the current events and cultural norms they are surrounded with. Poets often produce the most telling literature, giving insight into the society and mind-set they come from. This can be done in many forms.

The oldest types of poems often include many stanzas, may or may not rhyme, and are more about telling a story than experimenting with language or words. The most common types of ancient poetry are epics, which are usually extremely long stories that follow a hero through his journey, or ellegies, which are often solemn in tone and used to mourn or lament something or someone. The Mesopotamians are often said to have invented the written word, and their literature is among the oldest in the world, including the epic poem titled "Epic of Gilgamesh." Similar in style and length to "Gilgamesh" is "Beowulf," an ellegy written in Old English and set in Scandinavia. These poems are often used by professors as the earliest examples of literature.

The importance of poetry was revived in the Renaissance. At this time, Europeans discovered the style and beauty of ancient Greek arts, and poetry was among those. Shakespeare is the most well-known poet of the time, and he used poetry not only to write poems but also to write plays for the theater. The most popular forms of poetry during the Renaissance included villanelles, (a nineteen-line poetic form) sonnets, as well as the epic. Poets during this time focused on style and form, and developed very specific rules and outlines for how an exceptional poem should be written.

As often happens in the arts, modern poets have rejected the constricting rules of Renaissance poets, and free form poems are much more popular. Some modern poems would read just like stories if they weren't arranged into lines and stanzas. It is difficult to tell which poems and poets will be the most important, because works of art often become more famous in hindsight, after the poet has died and society can look at itself without being in the moment. Modern poetry continues to develop, and will no doubt continue to change as values, thought, and writing continue to change.

Poems can be among the most enlightening and uplifting texts for a person to read if they are looking to connect with the past, connect with other people, or try to gain an understanding of what is happening in their time.

27. In summary, the author has written this passage

a. as a foreword that will introduce a poem in a book or magazine

b. because she loves poetry and wants more people to like it

c. to give a brief history of poems

d. to convince students to write poems

28. The author organizes the paragraphs mainly by

a. moving chronologically, explaining which types of poetry were common in that time

b. talking about new types of poems each paragraph and explaining them a little

c. focusing on one poet or group of people and the poems they wrote

d. explaining older types of poetry so she can talk about modern poetry

29. The author's claim that poetry has been around "virtually from the time civilizations invented the written word" is supported by the detail that

a. Beowulf is written in Old English, which is not really in use any longer

b. epic poems told stories about heroes

c. the Renaissance poets tried to copy Greek poets

d. the Mesopotamians are credited with both inventing the word and writing "Epic of Gilgamesh"

30. According to the passage, the word "telling" means

a. speaking

b. significant

c. soothing

d. wordy

Verbal Ability Part II – Vocabulary

31. Choose a verb that means fearless or invulnerable to intimidation and fear.

a. Feeble
b. Strongest
c. Dauntless
d. Super

32. Choose a word that means the same as the underlined word.

I see the differences when they are placed side-by-side and <u>juxtaposed.</u>

a. Compared
b. Eliminated
c. Overturned
d. Exonerated

33. Choose the best definition of regicide.

a. v. To endow or furnish with requisite ability, character, knowledge and skill
b. n. killing of a king
c. adj. Disposed to seize by violence or by unlawful or greedy methods
d. v. To refresh after labor

34. Choose the best definition of pernicious.

a. Deadly
b. Infectious
c. Common
d. Rare

35. Fill in the blank.

After she received her influenza vaccination, Nan thought that she was ________ to the common cold.

a. Immune
b. Susceptible
c. Vulnerable
d. At risk

36. Choose a word that means the same as the underlined word.

She performed the gymnastics and stretches so well! I have never seen anyone so <u>nimble</u>.

a. Awkward
b. Agile
c. Quick
d. Taut

37. Choose a word that means the same as the underlined word.

Are there any more <u>queries</u>? We have already had so many questions today.

a. Questions
b. Commands
c. Obfuscations
d. Paradoxes

38. Choose a verb that means to remove a leader or high official from position.

a. Sack
b. Suspend
c. Depose
d. Dropped

39. Choose the best definition of pedestrian.

a. Rare
b. Often
c. Walking or Running
d. Commonplace

40. Choose the best definition of petulant.

a. Patient
b. Childish
c. Impatient
d. Mature

41. Fill in the blank.

Paul's rose bushes were being destroyed by Japanese beetles, so he invested in a good _______.

a. Fungicide
b. Fertilizer
c. Sprinkler
d. Pesticide

42. Choose the best definition of salient.

a. v. To make light by fermentation, as dough
b. adj. Not stringent or energetic
c. adj. negligible
d. adj. worthy of note or relevant

43. Choose the best definition of sedentary.

a. n. A morbid condition, due to obstructed excretion of bile or characterized by yellowing of the skin
b. adj. not moving or sitting at a place
c. v. To wander from place to place
d. n. Perplexity

44. Fill in the blank.

The last time that the crops failed, the entire nation experienced months of ________.

a. Famine
b. Harvest
c. Plenitude
d. Disease

45. Choose the best definition of stint.

a. Thrifty
b. Annoyed
c. Dislike
d. Insult

46. Choose the best definition of precipitate.

a. To rain
b. To throw down
c. To throw up
d. to snow

47. Choose the verb that means to build up or strengthen relative to morals or religion.

a. Sanctify
b. Amplify
c. Edify
d. Wry

48. Choose the noun that means exit or way out.

a. Door-jamb
b. Egress
c. Regress
d. Furtherance

49. Choose the best definition of the underlined word.

The tide was in this morning but now it is starting to <u>recede</u>.

a. Go out
b. Flow
c. Swell
d. Come in

50. Choose the word that means private, personal.

a. Confidential
b. Hysteric
c. Simplistic
d. Promissory

51. Choose the best definition of the underlined word.

I don't think that will make it any better - it is just going to <u>aggravate</u> the situation.

a. Worsen
b. Precipitate
c. Elongate
d. None of the above

52. Choose the best definition of the underlined word.

I didn't think this was her first appearance, but it is her <u>debut</u>.

a. Exit
b. Introduction
c. Curtain Call
d. Resignation

53. Fill in the blank.

Because of a pituitary dysfunction, Karl lacked the necessary _________ to grow as tall as his father.

a. Glands
b. Hormones
c. Vitamins
d. Testosterone

54. Choose the best definition of importune.

a. To find an opportunity
b. To ask all the time
c. Cannot find an opportunity
d. None of the above

55. Choose the best definition of sedulous.

a. n. The support on or against which a lever rests
b. adj. constant steady pursuit
c. v. To oppose with an equal force
d. n. The branch of medical science that relates to improving health

56. Choose the best definition of tincture.

a. n. alcoholic drink with plant extract used for medicine
b. n. An artificial trance-sleep
c. n. a special medicinal drink made by mixing water with plant extracts
d. adj. the point of puncture

57. Choose the noun that means serious criminal offence that is punishable by death or imprisonment above a year

a. Trespass
b. Hampers
c. Felony
d. Obligatory

58. Choose the best meaning of the underlined word.

His library is enormous. I didn't realize he was such a bibliophile.

a. Book lover
b. Audiophile
c. Bibliophobe
d. Audiophobe

59. Fill in the blank.

When Mr. Davis returned from southern Asia, he told us about the ________ that sometimes swept the area, bringing torrential rain.

a. Monsoons
b. Hurricanes
c. Blizzards
d. Floods

60. Choose the best definition of volatile.

a. Not explosive
b. Catches fire easily
c. Does not catch fire
d. Explosive

Section II – Math

1. What is 1/3 of 3/4?

a. 1/4
b. 1/3
c. 2/3
d. 3/4

2. What fraction of $1500 is $75?

a. 1/14
b. 3/5
c. 7/10
d. 1/20

3. Add $-3x^2 + 2x + 6$ and $-x^2 - x - 1$.

a. $-2x^2 + x + 5$
b. $-4x^2 + x + 5$
c. $-2x^2 + 3x + 5$
d. $-4x^2 + 3x + 5$

4. 3.14 + 2.73 + 23.7 =

a. 28.57
b. 30.57
c. 29.56
d. 29.57

5. Find the mean of these set of numbers: 200,000, 10,020, 30,000, 15,000 1080

a. 1080
b. 15,000
c. 256,100
d. 51,220

6. What is 0.27 + 0.33 expressed as a fraction?

a. 3/6
b. 4/7
c. 3/5
d. 2/7

7. What is (3.13 + 7.87) X 5?

a. 65
b. 50
c. 45
d. 55

8. Express 3^4 in standard form

a. 81
b. 27
c. 12
d. 9

9. What is 2/4 X 3/4 reduced to lowest terms?

a. 6/12
b. 3/8
c. 6/16
d. 3/4

10. If a = 2 and y = 5, solve $xy^3 - x^3$

a. 240
b. 258
c. 248
d. 242

11. Three tenths of 90 equals:

a. 18
b. 45
c. 27
d. 36

12. Find the mean of these set of numbers: 1, 2, 3, 4, 5, 6, 7, 8, 9, 10

a. 55
b. 5.5
c. 11
d. 10

13. .4% of 36 equals

a. 1.44
b. .144
c. 14.4
d. 144

14. 5x + 3 = 7x -1. Find x

a. 1/3
b. 1/2
c. 1
d. 2

15. Find 2 numbers that sum to 21 and the sum of the squares is 261.

a. 14 and 7
b. 15 and 6
c. 16 and 5
d. 17 and 4

16. 5x + 2(x + 7) = 14x – 7. Find x

a. 1
b. 2
c. 3
d. 4

17. 5(z + 1) = 3(z + 2) + 11. Find z

a. 2
b. 4
c. 6
d. 12

18. What are the prime factors of 81?

a. 3 x 3 x 9
b. 3 x 27
c. 3 x 3 x 3 x 3
d. All of the above

19. The price of a book went up from $20 to $25. What percent did the price increase?

a. 5%
b. 10%
c. 20%
d. 25%

20. After taking several practice tests, Brian improved the results of his GRE test by 30%. Given that the first time he took the test Brian answered 150 questions correctly, how many questions did he answer correctly on the second test?

a. 105
b. 120
c. 180
d. 195

21. Simplify $4^3 + 2^4$

a. 45
b. 108
c. 80
d. 48

22. A square lawn has an area of 62,500 square meters. How much will it cost to build a fence around it at a rate of $5.5 per meter?

a. $4000
b. $4500
c. $5000
d. $5500

23. A javelin is thrown into a field at 18m/s. if the Javelin weighs 1.5kg, what is the momentum?

a. 1.2 kg x m/s into the field
b. 12 kg x m/s into the field
c. 27 kg x m/s into the field
d. 2.7 kg x m/s into the field

24. Convert 204 to scientific notation

a. 2.04×10^{-2}

b. 0.204×10^{2}

c. 2.04×10^{3}

d. 2.04×10^{2}

25. There are 15 yellow and 35 orange balls in a basket. How many yellow balls must be added to make the yellow balls 65%?

a. 35

b. 50

c. 65

d. 70

26. If 144 students need to go on a trip and the buses each carry 36 students, how many buses are needed?

a. 2

b. 3

c. 4

d. 4.5

27. Using the factoring method, solve the quadratic equation: $x^2 + 4x + 4 = 0$

a. 0 and 1

b. 1 and 2

c. 2

d. -2

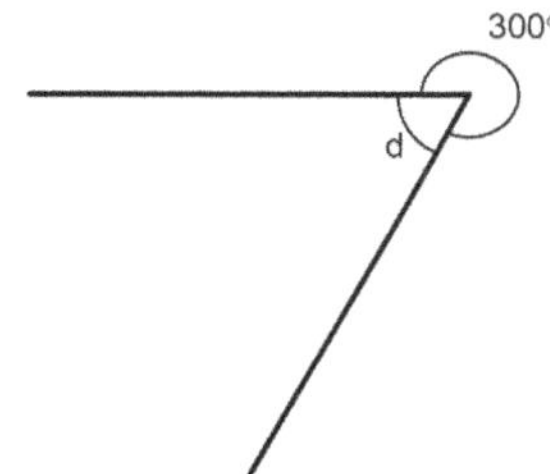

28. What is the measurement of the indicated angle?

a. 45°
b. 90°
c. 60°
d. 50°

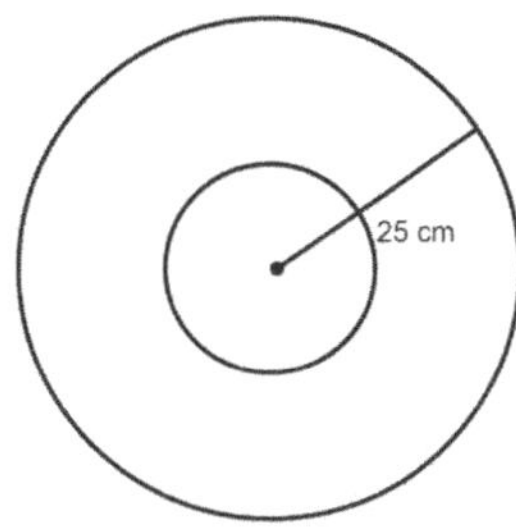

Note: figure not drawn to scale

29. What is the distance traveled by the wheel above, when it makes 175 revolutions?

a. 87.5 π m
b. 875 π m
c. 8.75 π m
d. 8750 π m

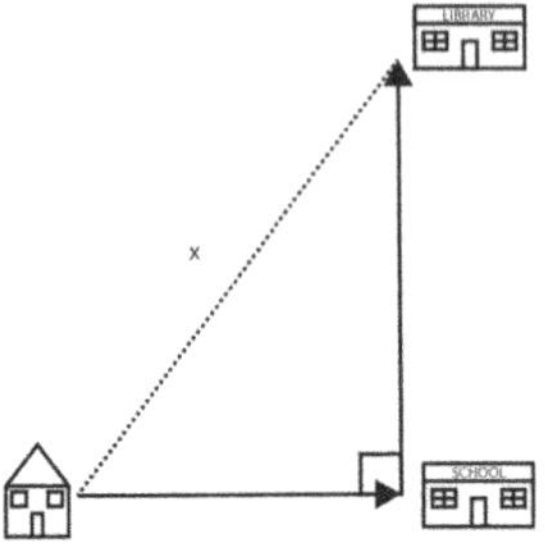

Note: figure not drawn to scale

30. Every day starting from his home Peter travels due east 3 kilometers to the school. After school he travels due north 4 kilometers to the library. What is the distance between Peter's home and the library?

a. 15 km
b. 10 km
c. 5 km
d. 12 ½ km

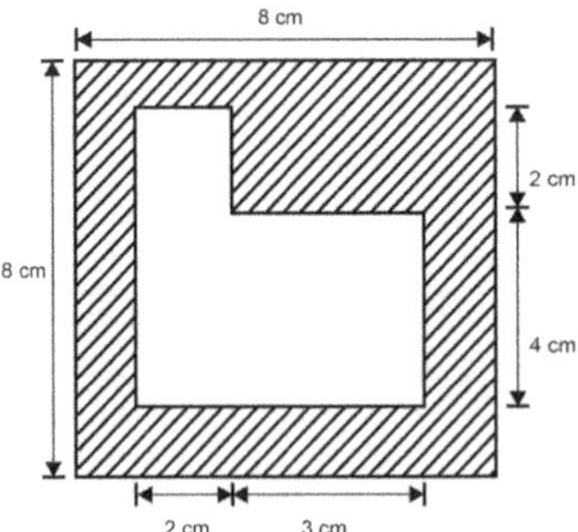

Note: figure not drawn to scale

31. What is the area of the shaded region in the figure above?

a. 64 cm^2
b. 44 cm^2
c. 60 cm^2
d. 40 cm^2

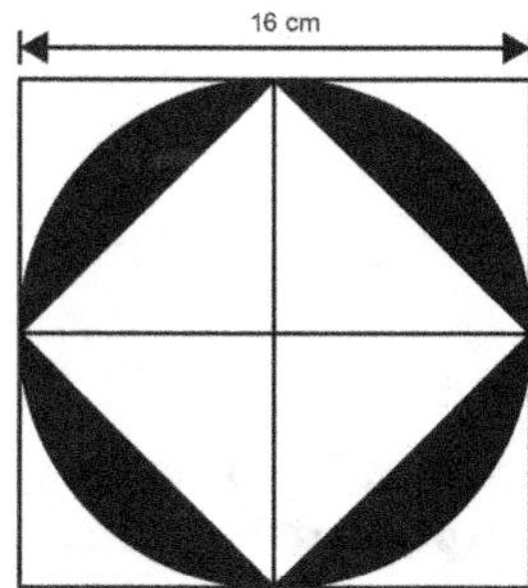

Note: figure not drawn to scale

32. A tile factory makes custom tiles, shown above, from two types of stone. If a customer requires 200 tiles, how much black stone will be required?

a. 256 m^2
b. 2560 m^2
c. 2.56 m^2
d. 25.6 m^2

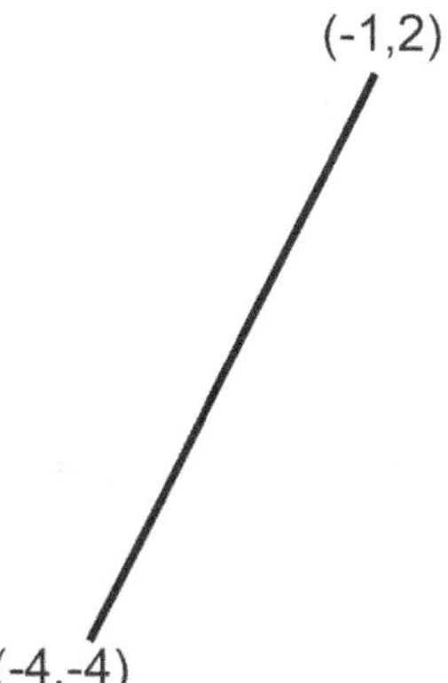

33. What is the slope of the line above?

a. 1
b. 2
c. 3
d. -2

34. A caterer is hired for a wedding and needs to calculate how much wine is needed. The couple for her weddings always gets two liters of wine. Each guest receives 0.20 liters. If y is the amount of wine needed in total liters, and if x is the number of wedding guests, which equation below should be used calculate the number of liters the caterer will need?

a. y = 0.20x + 2
b. y = 2x + 0.20
c. y = 2.20x
d. x = 0.20y + 2

35. If we know it takes 12 men to operate four machines, how many are required for 20 machines?

a. 6
b. 20
c. 60
d. 9

36. Brad has agreed to buy everyone a Coke. Each drink costs $1.89, and there are 5 friends. Estimate Brad's cost.

a. $7
b. $8
c. $10
d. $12

37. An object that weighs 500g is rolling along the road at 3.5m/s, what is the momentum of the object?

a. 124.9 kg x m/s along road
b. 17. 50 kg x m/s along road
c. 1750 kg x m/s along road
d. 1.75 kg x m/s along road

38. Solve √121

a. 11
b. 12
c. 21
d. None of the above

39. What are the prime factors of 25?

a. 4 x 5.5
b. 5 x 5 x 5
c. 1 x 25
d. 5 x 5

40. Convert 0.00002011 to scientific notation

a. 2.011×10^{-4}
b. 2.011×10^{5}
c. 2.011×10^{-6}
d. 2.011×10^{-5}

41. Express the ratio of 7:25 as a percentage.

a. 20%
b. 22%
c. 25%
d. 28%

42.

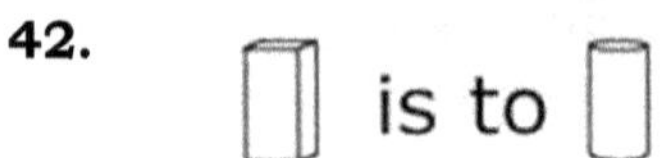

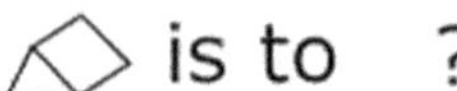

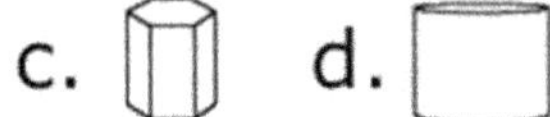

43.

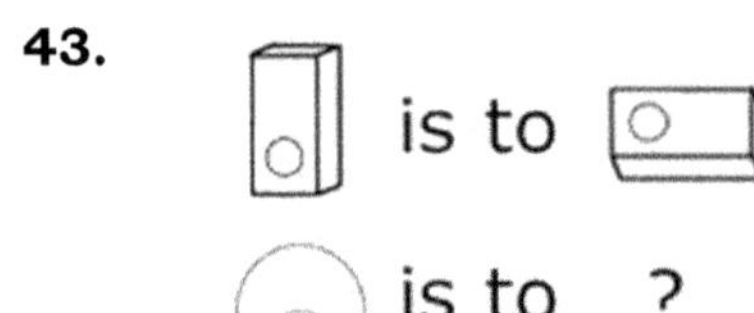

a. b.

c. d.

44.

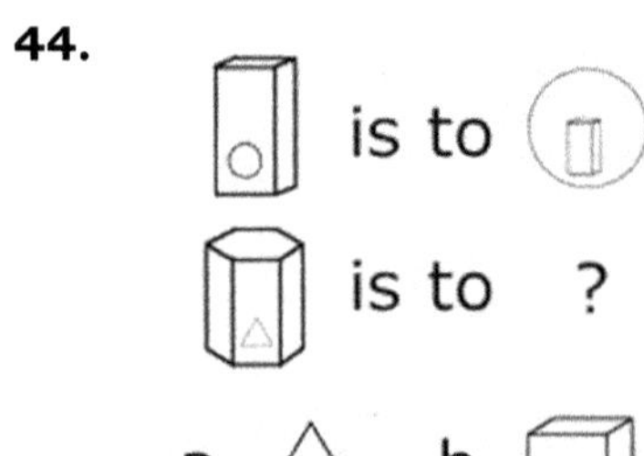

c. d.

45. Simplify the following expression:

$3x^3 + 2x^2 + 5x - 7 + 4x^2 - 5x + 2 - 3x^3$

a. $6x^2 - 9$

b. $6x^2 - 5$

c. $6x^2 - 10x - 5$

d. $6x^2 + 10x - 9$

46. A building is 15 m long and 20 m wide and 10 m high. What is the volume of the building?

a. 45 m^3

b. 3,000 m^3

c. 1500 m^3

d. 300 m^3

47. What is 465,890 less 456,890?

a. 9,000

b. 7000

c. 8970

d. 8500

48. Solve 3/4 + 2/4 + 1.2

a. 1 1/7

b. 2 3/4

c. 2 9/20

d. 3 1/4

49. A map uses a scale of 1:2,000. How much distance on the ground is 5.2 inches on the map if the scale is in inches?

a. 100,400
b. 10, 500
c. 10,440
d. 10,400

50. A bag contains 38 black balls and 42 white balls. What is the ratio of black balls to white?

a. 9:11
b. 1:3
c. 19:21
d. 11:9

Section III – Science

1. A motorcycle is travelling at 90 mph accelerates to pass a truck. Five seconds later, it is going 120 mph. Calculate the motorcycles' acceleration

a. 6 mph/second^2
b. 10 mph/second^2
c. 15 mph/second^2
d. 20 mph/second^2

2. Which of the following disciplines have a close relationship with cell biology?

a. Genetics
b. Genealogy
c. Paleontology
d. Archaeology

3. A solution with a pH value of greater than 7 is

a. Base
b. Acid
c. Neutral
d. None of the above

4. Ohm's law states

a. The voltage across a resistor is not equal to the product of the resistance and the current flowing through it.
b. The voltage across a resistor is equal to the product of the resistance and the current flowing through it.
c. The voltage across a resistor is greater than the product of the resistance.
d. The voltage across a resistor is equal to the current flowing through it.

5. Which statement below regarding Eukaryotic and prokaryotic cells is correct?

a. Both are organelles
b. Eukaryotic are not organelles
c. Both have DNA
d. Both have single membrane compartments

6. Electricity is a general term encompassing a variety of phenomena resulting from the presence and flow of electric charge. Which of the following statements about electricity is/are true?

a. Electrically charged matter is influenced by, and produces, electromagnetic fields.
b. Electric current is a movement or flow of electrically charged particles.
c. Electric potential is a fundamental interaction between the magnetic field and the presence and motion of an electric charge.
d. An influence produced by an electric charge on other charges in its vicinity is an electric field.

7. Which of these is not a process involved in cellular biology?

a. Active transport
b. Adhesion
c. Subversion
d. Cell signaling

8. When we say that important traits for scientific classification are homologous, "homologous" means

a. Being shared among two or more animals with the same parent.
b. Being coincidentally shared by two totally different creatures.
c. Being inherited by the organisms' common ancestors.
d. Mutating beyond all reasonable expectations.

9. The manner in which instructions for building proteins, the basic structural molecules of living material are written in the DNA, is

a. Genotypic assignment
b. Chromosome pattern
c. Genetic code
d. Genetic fingerprinting

10. A ______ is a unit of inherited material, encoded by a strand of DNA and transcribed by RNA.

a. Allele
b. Phenotype
c. Gene
d. Genotype

11. A runner can sprint 6 meters per second. How far will she travel in 2 minutes?

a. 600 meters
b. 720 meters
c. 760 meters
d. 800 meters

12. Which of these is not an area studied in cell biology?

a. Cells physiological properties
b. Cell structure
c. Cell life cycle
d. Cellular scientists' biographies

13. Why is detection of pathogens complicated?

a. They evolve so quickly
b. They die so quickly
c. They are invisible
d. They multiply so quickly

14. Calculate the molarity of a sugar solution if 4 liters of the solution contains 8 moles of sugar?

a. 0.5 M
b. 8 M
c. 2 M
d. 80 M

15. Which of the following is/are not included in Ohm's Law?

a. Ohm's Law defines the relationships between (P) power, (E) voltage, (I) current, and (R) resistance.

b. One ohm is the resistance value through which one volt will maintain a current of one ampere.

c. Using Ohm's Law, voltage is determined using V = IR, with I equaling current and R equaling resistance.

d. An ohm (Ω) is a unit of electrical voltage.

16. How many elements are represented on the modern periodic table?

a. 122 elements

b. 99 elements

c. 102 elements

d. 118 elements

17. Which, if any, of the following statements are false?

a. A mutation is a permanent change in the DNA sequence of a gene.

b. Mutations in a gene's DNA sequence can alter the amino acid sequence of the protein encoded by the gene.

c. Mutations in DNA sequences usually occur spontaneously.

d. Mutations in DNA sequences can caused by exposure to environmental agents such as sunshine.

18. Three cars are travelling down an even road at a velocity of 110 m/s, calculate the car with the highest momentum if they are all moving at the same speed, but the first car weighs 2500 kg, second car weighs 2650 kg and third car weighs 2009 kg?

a. First car

b. Second car

d. Third car

d. All have same momentum

19. Starting with the weakest, arrange the fundamental forces of nature in order of strength.

a. Gravity, Weak Nuclear Force, Electromagnetic Force, Strong Nuclear Force

b. Weak Nuclear Force, Gravity, Electromagnetic Force, Strong Nuclear Force

c. Strong Nuclear Force, Weak Nuclear Force, Electromagnetic Force, Gravity

d. Gravity, Strong Nuclear Force, Weak Nuclear Force, Electromagnetic Force

20. What are electrons?

a. Subatomic particles that carry a negative charge

b. Subatomic particles that carry a positive charge

c. Subatomic particles that carry both a negative and positive charge

d. None of the above

21. Cell culture is defined as

a. The technique for growing cells independent of a living organism within the confines of a laboratory.

b. The process of killing cells through use of lasers.

c. The method of creating cellular communities.

d. A method for localizing proteins in tissue slices.

22. ________, which refers to the repeatability of measurement, does not require knowledge of the correct or true value.

a. Precision

b. Value

c. Certainty

d. Accuracy

23. How much force is needed to accelerate a car weighing 2,000 kg, at a rate of 3 m/s^2?

a. 6000 N

b. 10,000 N

c. 4000 N

d. 8000 N

24. Describe the periodic table.

a. The periodic table is a tabular display of the chemical compounds organized by their atomic numbers, electron configurations, and recurring chemical properties.

b. The periodic table is a tabular display of the chemical elements, organized by their atomic numbers, electron configurations, and recurring chemical properties.

c. The periodic table is a tabular display of the chemical subatomic particles, organized by their atomic numbers, electron configurations, and recurring chemical properties.

d. None of the above.

25. The scientific discipline that studies the physiological aspects, structures, life cycles and division of cells is called _________.

a. Physiology
b. Cell science
c. Biochemistry
d. Cell biology

26. What is the minimum amount of energy required to remove an electron from an atom or ion in the gas phase?

a. Ionization energy
b. Valence energy
c. Atomic energy
d. Ionic energy

27. In a redox reaction, the number of electrons lost is

a. Less than the number of electrons gained
b. More than the number of electrons gained
c. Equal to the number of electrons gained
d. None of the above

28. In terms of the scientific method, the term ___________ refers to the act of noticing or perceiving something and/or recording a fact or occurrence.

a. Observation
b. Diligence
c. Perception
d. Control

29. The ______ Theory defines acids and bases in terms of the electron-pair concept; according to its definition, an acid is an electron-pair acceptor, and a base is an electron-pair donor.

a. Arrhenius

b. Lewis

c. Clark

d. Brønstead-Lowry

30. What is the molarity of a solution containing 5 moles of solute in 250 milliliters of solution?

a. 20 M

b. 15 M

c. 0.104 M

d. 1.25 M

31. The property of a conductor that restricts its internal flow of electrons is:

a. Friction

b. Power

c. Current

d. Resistance

32. Describe bacteria.

a. Prokaryotic microorganisms that are usually just a few micrometers long.

b. A single-celled organism.

c. A virus.

d. Three or more molecules clumped together.

33. What is the difference, of any, between kinetic energy and potential energy?

a. Kinetic energy is the energy of a body that results from heat while potential energy is the energy possessed by an object that is chilled.

b. Kinetic energy is the energy of a body that results from motion while potential energy is the energy possessed by an object by virtue of its position or state, e.g., as in a compressed spring.

c. There is no difference between kinetic and potential energy; all energy is the same.

d. Potential energy is the energy of a body that results from motion while kinetic energy is the energy possessed by an object by virtue of its position or state, e.g., as in a compressed spring.

34. A rocket releases a satellite into orbit around Earth. The satellite travels at 2000 m/s in 25 seconds. What is the acceleration?

a. 60 m/sec^2

b. 80 m/sec^2

c. 100 m/sec^2

d. 120 m/sec^2

35. Name the four states in which matter exists.

a. Concrete, liquid, gas, and plasma

b. Solid, fluid, gas, and plasma

c. Solid, liquid, vapor, and plasma

d. Solid, liquid, gas, and plasma

36. Which one of the following best describes the function of a cell membrane?

a. It controls the substances entering and leaving the cell.

b. It keeps the cell in shape.

c. It controls the substances entering the cell.

d. It supports the cell structures

37. Describe electric current.

a. Electric current is the flow of voltage

b. Electric current is the movement of negative ions.

c. Electric current is the flow of electric charge through a medium.

d. None of the above

38. Which of the following is not a typical shape for a bacterium?

a. Rod

b. Spiral

c. Sphere

d. Cube

39. What is usually the result when acid reacts with most of the metals?

a. Carbon dioxide

b. Oxygen gas

c. Nitrogen gas

d. Hydrogen gas

40. Which of these is not a rank within the area of classification or taxonomy?

a. Species
b. Family
c. Genus
d. Relative position

41. Which of the following statements about the periodic table of the elements is true?

a. On the periodic table, the elements are arranged according to their atomic mass.
b. The way in which the elements are arranged allows for predictions to made about their behavior.
c. The vertical columns of the table are called rows.
d. The horizontal rows of the table are called groups.

42. The scientific term ___________ refers to a practical test designed with the intention that its results be relevant to a particular theory or set of theories.

a. Procedure
b. Variable
c. Hypothesis
d. Experiment

43. Substances that deactivate catalysts are called

a. Inhibitors
b. Catalytic poisons
c. Positive catalysts
d. None of the above

44. What is the force per unit area exerted against a surface by the weight of air above that surface in the Earth's atmosphere?

a. Gravitational force
b. Atmospheric pressure
c. Barometric density
d. Aneroid pressure

45. Describe kinetic energy.

a. Kinetic energy is the energy an object possesses due to its mass.
b. Kinetic energy is the energy an object possesses due to its motion.
c. Kinetic energy is the energy an object possesses due to its chemical properties.
d. Kinetic energy is the stored energy an object possesses.

46. Another term for biological classification is:

a. Darwinian classification
b. Animal classification
c. Molecular classification
d. Scientific classification

47. When do oxidation and reduction reactions occur?

a. One after the other
b. In separate reactions
c. On the product side of the reaction
d. Simultaneously

48. What type of gene is not expressed as a trait unless inherited by both parents?

a. Principal gene
b. Latent gene
c. Recessive gene
d. Dominant gene

49. A ________ _______ is an approximation or simulation of a real system that omits all but the most essential variables of the system.

a. Scientific method
b. Independent variable
c. Control group
d. Scientific model

50. How many moles of Na are needed to make 4.5 liters of a 1.5 M Na solution?

a. 3 mol
b. 0.33 M
c. 0.33 mol
d. 3 M

51. Neutrons are necessary within an atomic nucleus because

a. They bind with protons via nuclear force
b. They bind with nuclei via nuclear force
c. They bind with protons via electromagnetic force
d. They bind with nuclei via electromagnetic force

52. How do atoms of different elements combine to form chemical mixtures?

a. Atoms of different elements combine in simple whole-number ratios to form chemical compounds.

b. Atoms of different components combine in simple fractional ratios to form chemical compounds.

c. Atoms of the same element combine in simple whole-number ratios to form chemical compounds.

d. Atoms of different elements combine in simple whole-number ratios to form chemical mixtures.

53. Which of the following statements is false?

a. Most enzymes are proteins

b. Enzymes are catalysts

c. Most enzymes are inorganic

d. Enzymes are large biological molecules

54. _________ are compounds that contain hydrogen, can dissolve in water to release hydrogen ions into solution, and, in an aqueous solution, can conduct electricity.

a. Caustics

b. Bases

c. Acids

d. Salts

55. Find the momentum of a round stone weighing 12.05 kg rolling down a hill at 8 m/s.

a. 95 kg m/sec down the hill.

b. 96.4 kg m/sec down the hill.

c. 100 kg m/sec down the hill.

d. 90 kg m/sec down the hill.

56. Which of the following statements about non-metals are false?

a. A non-metal is a substance that conducts heat and electricity poorly.

b. Most known chemical elements are non-metals.

c. A non-metal is brittle or waxy or gaseous.

d. None of the statements are false.

57. What is the name of the discipline that studies bacteria?

a. Bacteriography

b. Bacteriology

c. Bacteriepathy

d. Bacterioscopy

58. What are the basic structural units of nucleic acids (DNA or RNA) whose sequence determines individual hereditary characteristics?

a. Gene

b. Nucleotide

c. Phosphate

d. Nitrogen base

59. Which of these statements about light energy is/are true?

a. Light consists of electromagnetic waves in the visible range.

b. The fundamental particle or quantum of light is a photon.

c. A and B are true.

d. None of the statements are true.

60. List the classifications of organisms in order of size.

a. Genus, Kingdom, Phylum/division, Class, Order, and Family Species

b. Order, Kingdom, Phylum/division, Genus, Class, and Family Species

c. Genus, Kingdom, Phylum/division, Class, Order, and Family Species

d. Kingdom ,Genus, Phylum/division, Class, Order, and Family Species

e. Family species, Order, Class, Phylum/division, Kingdom, and Genus

61. Explain chemical bonds.

a. Chemical bonds are attractions between atoms that form chemical substances containing two or more atoms.

b. Chemical bonds are attractions between protons that form chemical elements containing two or more atoms.

c. Chemical bonds are two or more atoms that form chemical substances.

d. None of the above

62. The number of protons in the nucleus of an atom is the

a. Atomic mass.

b. Atomic weight.

c. Atomic number.

d. None of the above.

63. The molarity of an aqueous solution of CaCl is defined as the

a. moles of CaCl per milliliter of solution
b. grams of CaCl per liter of water
c. grams of CaCl per milliliter of solution
d. moles of CaCl per liter of solution

64. An electron is:

a. A tiny particle with a negative charge.
b. A tiny particle with a positive charge.
c. A tiny particle with a negative charge that orbits a nucleus.
d. A tiny particle with a positive charge that orbits an atom.

65. What law states that, in a chemical change, energy can be neither created nor destroyed, but only changed from one form to another?

a. The Law of the Preservation of Matter
b. The Law of the Conservation of Energy
c. The Law of the Conservation of Energy
d. The Law of the Conservation of Energy

66. What is the simplest unit of any compound?

a. Atom
b. Proton
c. Molecule
d. Compound

67. Sex chromosomes are designated as being "X" or "Y" chromosomes. In terms of sex chromosomes, what differences exist between males and females?

a. Females have two X chromosomes and males have one X chromosome and one Y chromosome.

b. Females have one X chromosome, and males have one X chromosome and one Y chromosome.

c. Females have one Y chromosome, while males have one X chromosome.

d. Females have one X chromosome and one Y chromosome, and males have two X chromosomes.

68. A biofilm is

a. A dense aggregation of bacteria attached to surfaces.
b. A type of bacteria which causes disease.
c. A cluster of bacteria which is healthy to consume.
d. Bacteria which aids in digestion.

69. Identify the chemical properties of water.

a. Water has two hydrogen atoms covalently bonded to one oxygen atom.

b. Water has two oxygen atoms covalently bonded to one hydrogen atom.

c. Water has two hydrogen atoms polar covalently bonded to one oxygen atom.

d. Water has two oxygen atoms polar covalently bonded to one hydrogen atom.

70. Which of the following is not true of atomic theory?

a. Originated 2500 years ago with Greek philosopher, Leucippus and his pupil Democritus

b. Is the field of physics that describes the characteristics and properties of atoms that make up matter.

c. Explains temperature as the momentum of atoms.

d. Explains macroscopic phenomenon through the behavior of microscopic atoms.

71. Calculate the molarity of 2.5 liters of a lithium fluoride, LiF solution that contains 52 grams of LiF. (Gram-formula - atomic mass =26 grams/mole)

a. 0.8 M
b. 1.5 M
c. 0.5 mol
d. 2 mol

72. In physics, __________ is the force that opposes the relative motion of two bodies in contact.

a. Resistance
b. Abrasiveness
c. Friction
d. Antagonism

73. What is the difference between anabolism and catabolism?

a. Anabolism is the series of chemical reactions resulting in the synthesis of inorganic compounds, and catabolism is a series of chemical reactions that break down larger molecules.

b. Anabolism is the series of chemical reactions resulting in the synthesis of organic compounds, and catabolism is a series of chemical reactions that combine larger molecules.

c. Catabolism is the series of chemical reactions resulting in the synthesis of organic compounds, and anabolism is a series of chemical reactions that break down larger molecules.

d. Anabolism is the series of chemical reactions resulting in the synthesis of organic compounds, and catabolism is a series of chemical reactions that break down larger molecules.

74. What results when acid reacts with a base?

a. A weak acid
b. A weak base
c. A salt and water
d. Hydrogen

75. What is a reaction where an element gains electrons known as?

a. Reduction
b. Oxidation
c. Sublimation
d. Condensation

Answer Key

Section 1 – Verbal Ability

Part 1 – Reading Comprehension

1. A
Helen's parents hired Anne to teach Helen to communicate. Choice B is incorrect because the passage states Anne had trouble finding her way around, which means she could walk. Choice C is incorrect because you don't hire a teacher to teach someone to play. Choice D is incorrect because by age 6, if Helen had never eaten, she would have starved to death.

2. B
The correct answer because that fact is stated directly in the passage. The passage explains that Anne taught Helen to hear by allowing her to feel the vibrations in her throat.

3. A
We can infer that Anne is a patient teacher because she did not leave or lose her temper when Helen bit or hit her; she just kept trying to teach Helen. Choice B is incorrect because Anne taught Helen to read and talk. Choice C is incorrect because Anne could hear. She was partially blind, not deaf. Choice D is incorrect because it does not have to do with patience.

4. B
The passage states that it was hard for anyone but Anne to understand Helen when she spoke. Choice A is incorrect because the passage does not mention Helen spoke a foreign language. Choice C is incorrect because there is no mention of how quiet or loud Helen's voice was. Choice D is incorrect because we know from reading the passage that Helen did learn to speak.

5. D
This question tests the reader's summarization skills. The question is asking very generally about the message of the passage, and the title, "Ways Characters Communicate in

Theater," is one indication of that. The other choices A, B, and C are all directly from the text, and therefore readers may be inclined to select one of them, but are too specific to encapsulate the entirety of the passage and its message.

6. B

The paragraph on soliloquies mentions "To be or not to be," and it is from the context of that paragraph that readers may understand that because "To be or not to be" is a soliloquy, Hamlet will be introspective, or thoughtful, while delivering it. It is true that actors deliver soliloquies alone, and may be "solitary" (choice A), but "thoughtful" (choice B) is more true to the overall idea of the paragraph. Readers may choose C because drama and theater can be used interchangeably and the passage mentions that soliloquies are unique to theater (and therefore drama), but this answer is not specific enough to the paragraph in question. Readers may pick up on the theme of life and death and Hamlet's true intentions and select that he is "hopeless" (choice D), but those themes are not discussed either by this paragraph or passage, as a close textual reading and analysis confirms.

7. C

This question tests the reader's grammatical skills. Choice B seems logical, but parenthesis are actually considered to be a stronger break in a sentence than commas are, and along this line of thinking, actually disrupt the sentence more.

Choices A and D make comparisons between theater and film that are simply not made in the passage, and may or may not be true. This detail does clarify the statement that asides are most unique to theater by adding that it is not completely unique to theater, which may have been why the author didn't chose not to delete it and instead used parentheses to designate the detail's importance (choice C).

8. A

Low blood sugar occurs both in diabetics and healthy adults.

9. B

None of the statements are the author's opinion.

10. A
The author's purpose is the inform.

11. A
The only statement that is not a detail is, "A doctor can diagnosis this medical condition by asking the patient questions and testing."

12. A
This sentence is a recommendation.

13. C
Tips for a good night's sleep is the best alternative title for this article.

14. B
Mental activity is helpful for a good night's sleep is cannot be inferred from this article.

15. A
From the passage, one disadvantage of taking naps is they may keep you awake at night.

16. C
Based on the partial table of contents, you would find information about natural selection in the ecology section on page 110.

17. C
To be infamous means to be remembered for an evil or terrible action. Therefore, the word infamy means to remember a bad or terrible thing. Choice A is incorrect because being famous is not the same as being infamous. Choice B is incorrect because the attack on Pearl Harbor was not good. Choice D is incorrect because Pearl Harbor was not forgotten.

18. C
Each answer choice except choice C contains the name of at least one country that was not part of the AXIS powers.

19. D
It is stated in the passage. Choice A is not correct because

there was no indication that Japan would attack San Diego. Choice B is incorrect because the attack on Pearl Harbor was a surprise. Choice C is incorrect because Roosevelt was not planning to attack Japan.

20. C

The passage clearly states that Japan planned a surprise attack. They chose that early time to catch the U.S. military off guard. Choice A is incorrect because the military does not sleep late. Choice B is incorrect because there is no law against bombing countries. Choice D is incorrect because it makes no sense.

21. C

This question tests the reader's vocabulary skills. The uses of the negatives "but" and "less," especially right next to each other, may confuse readers into answering with choices A or D, which list words that are antonyms to "militant." Readers may also be confused by the comparison of healthy people with what is being described as an overly healthy person--both people are good, but the reader may look for which one is "worse" in the comparison, and therefore stray toward the antonym words. One key to understanding the meaning of "militant" if the reader is unfamiliar with it is to look at the root of the word; readers can then easily associate it with "military" and gain a sense of what the word signifies: defense (especially considered that the immune system defends the body). Choice C is correct over choice B because "militant" is an adjective, just as the words in choice C are, whereas the words in choice B are nouns.

22. C

This question tests the reader's understanding of function within writing. The other choices are details included surrounding the quoted text, and may therefore confuse the reader. A somewhat contradicts what is said earlier in the paragraph, which is that tests and treatments are improving, and probably doctors are along with them, but the paragraph doesn't actually mention doctors, and the subject of the question is the medicine. Choice B may seem correct to readers who aren't careful to understand that, while the author does mention the large number of people affected, the author is touching on the realities of living with allergies, rather than the likelihood of curing all allergies. Similarly, while the author does mention the "balance" of the body, which is easily associated with "wholesome," the author is not really making an argument and especially is not making an extreme statement that allergy medicines should be outlawed. Again, because the article's tone is on living with allergies, choice C is an appropriate choice that fits with the title and content of the text.

23. B

This question tests the reader's inference skills. The text does not state who is doing the recommending, but the use of the "patients," as well as the general context of the passage, lends itself to the logical partner, "doctors," choice B. The author does mention the recommendation but doesn't present it as her own (i.e. "I recommend that"), so choice A may be eliminated. It may seem plausible that people with allergies (choice D) may recommend medicines or products to other people with allergies, but the text does not necessarily support this interaction taking place. Choice C may be selected because the EpiPen is specifically mentioned, but the use of the phrase "such as" when it is introduced is not limiting enough to assume the recommendation is coming from its creators.

24. D

This question tests the reader's global understanding of the text. Choice D includes the main topics of the three body paragraphs, and isn't too focused on a specific aspect or quote from the text, as the other questions are, giving a skewed summary of what the author intended. The reader may be drawn to choice B because of the title of the passage and the use of words like "better," but the message of the passage is larger and more general than this.

25. B

Reading the document posted to the Human Resources website is optional.

26. B

The document is recommended changes and have not be implemented yet.

27. C

This question tests the reader's summarization skills. The use of the word "actually" in describing what kind of people poets are, as well as other moments like this, may lead readers to selecting choices B or D, but the author is more information than trying to persuade readers. The author gives no indication that she loves poetry (choice B) or that people, students specifically (D), should write poems. Choice A is incorrect because the style and content of this paragraph do not match those of a foreword; forewords usually focus on the history or ideas of a specific poem to introduce it more fully and help it stand out against other poems. The author here focuses on several poems and gives broad statements. Instead, she tells a kind of story about poems, giving three very broad time periods in which to discuss them, thereby giving a brief history of poetry, as choice C states.

28. A

This question tests the reader's summarization skills. Key words in the topic sentences of each of the paragraphs ("oldest," "Renaissance," "modern") should give the reader an idea that the author is moving chronologically. The opening and closing sentence-paragraphs are broad and talk generally. B seems reasonable, but epic poems are mentioned in two paragraphs, eliminating the idea that only new types of poems are used in each paragraph. Choice C is also easily eliminated because the author clearly mentions several different poets, groups of people, and poems. Choice D also seems reasonable, considering that the author does move from older forms of poetry to newer forms, but use of "so (that)" makes this statement false, for the author gives no indication that she is rushing (the paragraphs are about the same size) or that she prefers modern poetry.

29. D

This question tests the reader's attention to detail. The key word is "invented"--it ties together the Mesopotamians, who invented the written word, and the fact that they, as the inventors, also invented and used poetry. The other selections focus on other details mentioned in the passage, such as that the Renaissance's admiration of the Greeks (choice C) and that Beowulf is in Old English (choice A). Choice B may seem like an attractive answer because it is unlike the others and because the idea of heroes seems rooted in ancient and early civilizations.

30. B

This question tests the reader's vocabulary and contextualization skills. "Telling" is not an unusual word, but it may be used here in a way that is not familiar to readers, as an adjective rather than a verb in gerund form. A may seem like the obvious answer to a reader looking for a verb to match the use they are familiar with. If the reader understands that the word is being used as an adjective and that choice A is a ploy, they may opt to select choice D, "wordy," but it does not make sense in context. Choice C can be easily eliminated, and doesn't have any connection to the paragraph or passage. "Significant" (choice B) makes sense contextually, especially relative to the phrase "give insight" used later in the sentence.

Verbal Ability Part II - Vocabulary

31. C

Dauntless: adj. Invulnerable to fear or intimidation.

32. A

Juxtaposed: adj. Placed side-by-side, often for comparison or contrast.

33. B

Regicide: v. killing of a king.

34. A

Pernicious: adj. Causing much harm in a subtle way.

35. A

Immune: adj. Resistant to a particular infection or toxin owing to the presence of specific antibodies.

36. B

Nimble: adj. Quick and light in movement or action.

37. A
Queries: n. Questions or inquiries.

38. C
Depose: To remove (a leader) from (high) office, without killing the incumbent.

39. D
Pedestrian: Ordinary, dull; everyday; unexceptional.

40. B
Petulant: adj. Childishly irritable.

41. D
Pesticide: n. A substance used for destroying insects or other organisms harmful to cultivated plants or to animals.

42. D
Salient: adj. worthy or note or relevant.

43. B
Sedentary: adj. not moving or sitting in one place.

44. A
Famine: n. extreme scarcity of food.

45. A
Stint: n. To be sparing.

46. A
Precipitate: v. to rain.

47. C
Edify: v. To instruct or improve morally or intellectually.

48. B
Egress: n. An exit or way out.

49. A
Recede: v. To move back, to move away.

50. A
Confidential: adj. kept secret within a certain circle of persons; not intended to be known publicly.

51. A
Aggravate: v. to make worse, or more severe; to render less tolerable or less excusable; to make more offensive; to enhance; to intensify.

52. B
Debut: n. a performer's first-time performance to the public.

53. B
Hormones: n. A regulatory substance produced in an organism and transported in tissue fluids such as blood or sap to stimulate specific cells.

54. B
Importune: v. To harass with persistent requests.

55. B
Sedulous: adj. Showing dedication and diligence.

56. A
Tincture: n. alcoholic drink with plant extracts used for medicine.

57. C
Felony: n. Serious criminal offence that is punishable by death or imprisonment above a year.

58. A
Bibliophile: n. One who loves books.

59. A
Monsoons: n. The rainy season accompanying the wet monsoon.

60. D
Volatile: adj. Explosive.

Section II – Mathematics

1. A
1/3 X 3/4 = 3/12 = 1/4

2. D
75/1500 = 15/300 = 3/60 = 1/20

3. B

We remove the brackets and we group the variables by degrees.

$-4x^2 + x + 5$

$(-3x^2 + 2x + 6) + (-x^2 - x - 1) =$

$-3x^2 + 2x + 6 - x^2 - x - 1 =$

$-4x^2 + x + 5$

4. D
3.14 + 2.73 = 5.87 and 5.87 + 23.7 = 29.57

5. D
First add all the numbers 200,000 + 10,020 + 30,000 + 15,000 + 1080 = 256,100. Then divide by 5 (the number of data provided) = 256,100/5 = 51,220

6. C
0.27 + 0.33 = 0.6 = 60/100 = 3/5.

7. D
3.13 + 7.87 = 11 and 11 X 5 = 55

8. A
3 x 3 x 3 x 3 = 81

9. B
2/4 X 3/4 = 6/16, in lowest terms = 3/8

10. D
$2(5)^3 - (2)^3 = 2(125) - 8 = 250 - 8 = 242$

11. C
3/10 * 90 = 3 * 90/10 = 270/10 = 27

12. C
First add all the numbers 1 + 2 + 3 + 4 + 5 +6 + 7 +8 + 9 + 10 = 55. Then divide by 10 (the number of data provided) = 55/5 = 11

13. B
.4/100 * 36 = .4 * 36/100 = 14.4/100 = 0.144

14. D
To solve for x,
5x – 7x + 3 = -1
5x – 7x = -1 -3
-2x = -4
x = -4/ -2
x = 2

15. B
There are two statements made. This means that we can write two equations according to these statements:
The sum of two numbers are 21: x + y = 21

The sum of the squares is 261: $x^2 + y^2 = 261$

We are asked to find x and y.

Since we have the sums of the numbers and the sums of their squares; we can use the square formula of x + y, that is:

$(x + y)^2 = x^2 + 2xy + y^2$ ... Here, we can insert the known values x + y and $x^2 + y^2$:

$(21)^2 = 261 + 2xy$ ... Arranging to find xy:

441 = 261 + 2xy

441 - 261 = 2xy

180 = 2xy

xy = 180/2

xy = 90

We need to find two number which multiply to 90. Checking the answer choices, we see that in (b), 15 and 6 are given. 15•6 = 90. Also their squares sum up to 261 (152 + 62 = 225 + 36 = 261). So these two numbers satisfy the equation.

16. C
To solve for x, first simplify the equation
5x + 2x + 14 = 14x – 7
7x + 14 = 14x -7
7x – 14x + 14 = -7
7x – 14x = -7 – 14
-7x = -21
x = -21/-7
x=3

17. C
5z + 5 = 3z +6 + 11
5z -3z + 5 =6 + 11
5z – 3z = 6 + 11 -5
2z = 17 – 5
2z = 12
z= 12/2
z= 6

18. C
To make this easier break 81 to 9 x 9 and then find the prime factors of each of these prime numbers. The prime factors of 9 = 3 x 3 and the prime factors of 9 = 3 x 3 Prime factors of 81 = 3 x 3 x 3 x 3

19. D
Price increased by $5 ($25-$20). The percent increase is 5/20 x 100 = 5 x 5=25%

20. D
30/100 x 150 = 3 x 15 = 45 (increase in number of correct answers). So the number of correct answers in second test will be the number of correct answers in the first test plus the increase, which is, 150 + 45 = 195

21. C
(4 x 4 x 4) + (2 x 2 x 2 x 2) = 64 + 16 = 80

22. D
As the lawn is square, the length of one side will be the square root of the area. √62,500 = 250 meters. So, the perimeter is found by 4 times the length of the side of the square:

250 * 4 = 1000 meters.

Since each meter costs $5.5, the total cost of the fence will be 1000•5.5 = $5,500.

23. C
p = 1.5 x 18 = 27 kg x m/s into the field.

24. D
The decimal point moves 2 spaces right to be placed after 2, which is the first non-zero number. Thus it is 2.04 x 10^2

25. B
There are 50 balls in the basket now. Let x be the number of yellow balls that are to be added to make 65%. So the equation becomes
X + 15 /X + 50 = 65/100
X = 50

26. C
There are 144 students and each bus holds 36, so 144/36 = 4 buses.

27. D
$x^2 + 4x + 4 = 0$ ... We try to separate the middle term 4x to find common factors with x^2 and 4 separately:

$x^2 + 2x + 2x + 4 = 0$ ... Here, we see that x is a common factor for x^2 and 2x, and 2 is a common factor for 2x and 4:

x(x + 2) + 2(x + 2) = 0 ... Here, we have x times x + 2 and 2 times x + 2 summed up. This means that we have x + 2 times x + 2:

(x + 2)(x + 2) = 0

$(x + 2)^2 = 0$ ... This is true if only if x + 2 is equal to zero.

$x + 2 = 0$

$x = -2$

28. C

The sum of angles around a point is 360°
$d+300 = 360°$
$d = 60°$

29. A

The wheel travels 2πr distance when it makes one revolution. Here, r stands for the radius. The radius is given as 25 cm in the figure. So,

$2\pi r = 2\pi * 25 = 50\pi$ cm is the distance traveled in one revolution.

In 175 revolutions: $175 * 50\pi = 8750\pi$ cm is traveled.

We are asked to find the distance in meter.

1 m = 100 cm So;

8750π cm $= 8750\pi / 100 = 87.5\pi$ m

30. C

Pythagorean Theorem:
$(\text{Hypotenuse})^2 = (\text{Perpendicular})^2 + (\text{Base})^2$
$h^2 = a^2 + b^2$

Given: $3^2 + 4^2 = h^2$
$h^2 = 9 + 16$
$h = \sqrt{25}$
$h = 5$

31. D

Shaded area= Outer area – Inner area(square + rectangle)
Shaded area= (8 x 8) –{(2 x 2) + [(3 + 2) x 4]}, = 64 – (4 + 20), =
64- 24
Shaded area= 40 cm^2

32. A

Black stone for 200 tiles = 200 x [Total tile area – Inner white area(4 triangles)]

= 200 x [(162)-(4x1/2 x 8 x 8)] = 200 x (256-128) = 200 x 128
= 25600 cm^2
Converting to meters – 1 cm. = 0.01 meters
= 25600/100 m^2
= 256 m^2

33. B
If we know the coordinates of two points on a line, we can find the slope (m) with the below formula:

$m = (y_2 - y_1)/(x_2 - x_1)$ where (x_1, y_1) represent the coordinates of one point and (x_2, y_2) the other.

In this question:

(-4, -4) : $x_1 = -4$, $y_1 = -4$

(-1, 2) : $x_2 = -1$, $y_2 = 2$

Inserting these values into the formula:

m = (2 - (-4))/(-1 - (-4)) = (2 + 4)/(-1 + 4) = 6/3 ... Simplifying by 3:

m = 2

34. A
The equation for the total liters of wine will be y = 0.20x + 2

35. C
If it takes 12 men to operate four machines, then, 12 is to 4, as X is to 20. So X must be 3 X 20 = 60.

36. C
If there are 5 friends and each drink costs $1.89, we can round up to $2 per drink and estimate the total cost at, 5 X $2 = $10.

The actual cost is 5 X $1.89 = $9.45.

37. D
First convert 500g to kg = 500/1000 = 0.5kg, momentum = 0.5 x 3.5 = 1.75 kg x m/s along the road

38. A
√121

39. D

The smallest prime number that can divide 25 is 5. 25/5 = 5. Prime factors of 25 = 5 x 5

40. D

The decimal point moves 5 places left to be placed after 2, which is the first non-zero number. Thus its 2.011 x 10^{-5}

The answer is in the negative because the decimal moved left

41. D

7: 25 =X:100
25/7 = 3.5
100/3.5 = 28.5

42. B

The relation is two upright figures in the first set, and 2 horizontal figures in the second set.

43. C

The first pair contains a box with a circle inside, and the same figure on its side.

44. C

The inside and larger shapes are reversed.

45. B

$6x^2 - 5$
$3x^3 + 2x^2 + 5x - 7 + 4x^2 - 5x + 2 - 3x^3 = 6x^2 - 5$

46. B

Formula for volume of a shape is L x W x H = 15 x 20 x 10 = 3,000m^3

47. A

465,890 - 456,890 = 9,000

48. C

3/4 + 2/4 + 1.2, first convert the decimal to fraction, = 3/4 + 2/4 + 1 1/5 = ¾ + 2/4 + 6/5 = (find common denominator) (15 + 10 + 24)/20 = 49/20 = 2 9/20

49. D
1 inch on map = 2,000 inches on ground. So, 5.2 inches on map = 5.2 * 2,000 = 10,400 inches on ground.

50. C

The ratio of black balls to white is 38:42. Reduce to lowest terms = 19:21

Section III – Science

1. A
The formula for acceleration = A = $(V_f - V_0)/t$
so A = (120 -90)/5 sec = 6 mph/second^2

2. A
Only genetics pertains directly to the cell's function. For genetics, the cell of a new organism acquires traits of ancestral organisms.

3. A
A solution with a pH value of greater than 7 is base.

4. B
The voltage across a resistor is equal to the product of the resistance and the current flowing through it.

5. D
Both have single membrane compartments.

6. C
Electric potential is a fundamental interaction between the magnetic field and the presence and motion of an electric charge.

Electric potential is the capacity of an electric field to do work on an electric charge, typically measured in volts, while electromagnetism is a fundamental interaction between the magnetic field and the presence and motion of an electric charge.

7. C
Subversion. Active transport, adhesion and cell signaling are all involved in cellular biology.

8. C
Homologous is being inherited by the organisms' common ancestors. An example would be feathers and hair—both share a common ancestral trait.

9. C
The manner in which instructions for building proteins, the basic structural molecules of living material are written in the DNA is a **genetic code**.

10. C
A gene is a unit of inherited material, encoded by a strand of DNA and transcribed by RNA.

11. B
Speed = (total distance traveled)/(total time taken)
6 = x/120 (convert minutes to seconds)
6 * 120 = x
X = 720 meters

12. D
Cellular scientists' biographies are not studied in cell biology. The physiological properties of cells, cell structure and the life cycle of a cell are all valid topics of study within cell biology.

13. A
Detection of pathogens can be complicated because they evolve so quickly.

14. C
Molarity = moles of solute/liters of solution = 8/4 = 2

15. D
An ohm (Ω) is a unit of electrical voltage is not true.

Note: An ohm is a unit of electrical resistance.

16. D
The periodic table contains 118 elements.

17. C
Mutations in DNA sequences usually occur spontaneously is false.

18. C

Momentum is a product of velocity and mass. If they are all traveling at the same speed, the car that weighs the most would have the highest momentum.

19. A

Starting with the weakest, the fundamental forces of nature in order of strength are, Gravity, Weak nuclear force, Electromagnetic force, Strong nuclear force.

20. A

Electrons are subatomic particles that carry a negative charge.

21. A

Cell culture is the technique for growing cells independent of a living organism within the confines of a laboratory. The cell culture is generally grown in a test-tube environment or on a petri dish.

22. A

Precision, which refers to the repeatability of measurement, does not require knowledge of the correct or true value.

23. A

Force = Mass times Acceleration Measured in Newtons.
$F = 2000 \text{ kg} \times 3 \text{ m/sec}^2 = 6000 \text{ N}$

24. B

The periodic table is a tabular display of the chemical elements, organized on the basis of their atomic numbers, electron configurations, and recurring chemical properties.

25. D

The scientific discipline that studies the physiological aspects, structures, life cycles and division of cells is called cell biology.

26. A

Ionization energy is the minimum amount of energy required to remove an electron from an atom or ion in the gas phase.

27. C

Redox is a complete reaction comprising oxidation and reduction reactions that are each only half of the complete reaction. The same exact electrons lost in oxidation are what are gained in reduction.

28. A

In terms of the scientific method, the term **observation** refers to the act of noticing or perceiving something and/or recording a fact or occurrence.

29. B

The Lewis Theory defines acids and bases in terms of the electron-pair concept; according to its definition, an acid is an electron-pair acceptor, and a base is an electron-pair donor.

30. A

First convert 250 ml to liters, 250/1000 = 0.25 then calculate molarity = 5 moles/ 0.25 liters = 20 M.

31. D

The property of a conductor that restricts its internal flow of electrons is resistance.

32. A

Prokaryotic microorganisms that are usually just a few micrometers long.

33. B

Kinetic energy is the energy of a body that results from motion while potential energy is the energy possessed by an object by virtue of its position or state, e.g., as in a compressed spring.

34. B

The formula for acceleration = $A = (V_f - V_0)/t$
so $A = (2000 - 0)/25$ sec $= 80$ m/sec^2

35. A

The four states in which matter exists are solid, fluid, gas, and plasma.

The state of matter is determined by the strength of the bonds between the atoms that make up matter.

36. A

The cell membrane is a biological membrane that separates the interior of all cells from the outside environment. The cell membrane is selectively permeable to ions and organic molecules and controls the movement of substances in and out of cells.

37. C

Electric current is the flow of electric charge through a medium.

38. D

Cubes rarely occur naturally, especially in the micro world outside the human eye. True cubes are usually deliberately created.

39. D

All acids contain hydrogen. When acids react with most metals, the metals displace the hydrogen and hydrogen gas is produced.

40. D

Relative position. Ranks include Domain, Kingdom, Phylum, Class, Order, Family, Genus, and Species.

41. B

The following statements about the periodic table of the elements is true,

The way in which the elements are arranged allows for predictions to made about their behavior.

42. D

The scientific term **experiment** refers to a practical test designed with the intention that its results be relevant to a particular theory or set of theories.

43. B

Substances that deactivate catalysts are called catalytic poisons.

44. B

Atmospheric pressure is the force per unit area exerted against a surface by the weight of air above that surface in the Earth's atmosphere.

45. B

Kinetic energy is the energy an object possesses due to its motion.

46. D

Scientific classification. The two phrases are interchangeable, although the former seems to more accurately reflect the purpose of classification: to categorize biological units.

47. D

Oxidation and reduction reactions are each just half of a redox reaction and both occur simultaneously, because the exact electrons lost in oxidation is what is gained in reduction.

48. C

A recessive gene is not expressed as a trait unless inherited by both parents.

49. D

A **scientific model** is an approximation or simulation of a real system that omits all but the most essential variables of the system.

50. A

X/4.5 = 1.5, X = 4.5/1.5 = 3 mol.

51. A

Neutrons are necessary within an atomic nucleus as they bind with protons via the nuclear force.

52. A

Atoms of different elements combine in simple whole-number ratios to form chemical compounds.

53. C

The following statement is false - Most enzymes are inorganic.

54. C

Acids are compounds that contain hydrogen and can dissolve in water to release hydrogen ions into solution.

55. B

Formula - P= kg x m/s
= 12.05kg x 8m/s
= 96.4 kg x m/s down the hill.

Note that the final answer has the proper SI unit of momentum (kg x m/s) after it and it also mentions the direction of the movement.

56. D
All of the statements are true.

a. A non-metal is a substance that conducts heat and electricity poorly.

b. Most of the known chemical elements are non-metals.

c. A non-metal is brittle or waxy or gaseous.

57. B
The discipline that studies bacteria is Bacteriology.

58. A
Genes determine individual hereditary characteristics.

59. C
A and B are true.

a. Light consists of electromagnetic waves in the visible range.
b. The fundamental particle or quantum of light is a photon.

Note: Light energy is the only visible form of energy. A light bulb is a device that uses electrical energy to create electromagnetic energy in the form (in part) of visible light and heat.

60. A
The groups into which organisms are classified are called taxa and include, in order of size, Genus, Kingdom, Phylum/division, Class, Order, and Family Species.

61. A
Chemical bonds are attractions between atoms that form chemical substances containing two or more atoms.

62. C
In chemistry, the number of protons in the nucleus of an atom is known as the atomic number, which determines the chemical element to which the atom belongs.

63. D

The molarity of an aqueous solution of CaCl is defined as the moles of CaCl per liter of solution.

64. C

An electron is a tiny particle with a negative charge that orbits a nucleus.

65. C

The Law of the Conservation of Energy states that, in a chemical change, energy can be neither created nor destroyed, but only changed from one form to another.

66. A

An atom is the basic or fundamental unit of any matter or element.

67. A

Females have two X chromosomes and males have one X chromosome and one Y chromosome.

68. A

A biofilm is a dense aggregation of bacteria attached to surfaces. The density of these bacteria is based on many factors, such as environment, temperature, and how long they are left undisturbed.

69. A

Water has two hydrogen atoms covalently bonded to one oxygen atom.

70. C

Choice C (Atomic theory explains temperature as the momentum of atoms.) is incorrect because atomic theory explains temperature as the motion of atoms (faster = hotter), not the momentum. The momentum of atoms explains the outward pressure that they exert.

71. A

First convert LiF grams to moles = 52 x 1/26 = 2. Now Molarity = 2 moles/2.5 liters = 0.8 M

72. C

In physics, friction is the force that opposes the relative motion of two bodies in contact.

73. D

Anabolism is the series of chemical reactions resulting in the synthesis of organic compounds, and catabolism is a series of chemical reactions that break down larger molecules.

74. C

When an acid and a base react, they neutralize each other's properties to form salt and water.

75. A

Reduction is a reaction that usually involves the gain of electrons that were lost in an oxidation reaction.

Practice Test Questions Set 2

The questions below are not the same as you will find on the PAX [RN] - that would be too easy! And nobody knows what the questions will be and they change all the time. Below are general questions that cover the same subject areas as the PAX RN. So while the format and exact wording of the questions may differ slightly, and change from year to year, if you can answer the questions below, you will have no problem with the PAX RN.

For the best results, take this Practice Test as if it were the real exam. Set aside time when you will not be disturbed, and a location that is quiet and free of distractions. Read the instructions carefully, read each question carefully, and answer to the best of your ability.

Use the bubble answer sheets provided. When you have completed the Practice Test, check your answer against the Answer Key and read the explanation provided.

Do not attempt more than one set of practice test questions in one day. After completing the first practice test, wait two or three days before attempting the second set of questions.

Section I – Verbal Ability
Questions: 80 **Time:** 60 Minutes

Section II – Mathematics
Questions: 50 **Time:** 60 Minutes

Section III – Science
Questions: 75 **Time:** 60 minutes

Answer Sheet – Verbal Ability

1. (A)(B)(C)(D)	21. (A)(B)(C)(D)	41. (A)(B)(C)(D)	61. (A)(B)(C)(D)
2. (A)(B)(C)(D)	22. (A)(B)(C)(D)	42. (A)(B)(C)(D)	62. (A)(B)(C)(D)
3. (A)(B)(C)(D)	23. (A)(B)(C)(D)	43. (A)(B)(C)(D)	63. (A)(B)(C)(D)
4. (A)(B)(C)(D)	24. (A)(B)(C)(D)	44. (A)(B)(C)(D)	64. (A)(B)(C)(D)
5. (A)(B)(C)(D)	25. (A)(B)(C)(D)	45. (A)(B)(C)(D)	65. (A)(B)(C)(D)
6. (A)(B)(C)(D)	26. (A)(B)(C)(D)	46. (A)(B)(C)(D)	66. (A)(B)(C)(D)
7. (A)(B)(C)(D)	27. (A)(B)(C)(D)	47. (A)(B)(C)(D)	67. (A)(B)(C)(D)
8. (A)(B)(C)(D)	28. (A)(B)(C)(D)	48. (A)(B)(C)(D)	68. (A)(B)(C)(D)
9. (A)(B)(C)(D)	29. (A)(B)(C)(D)	49. (A)(B)(C)(D)	69. (A)(B)(C)(D)
10. (A)(B)(C)(D)	30. (A)(B)(C)(D)	50. (A)(B)(C)(D)	70. (A)(B)(C)(D)
11. (A)(B)(C)(D)	31. (A)(B)(C)(D)	51. (A)(B)(C)(D)	71. (A)(B)(C)(D)
12. (A)(B)(C)(D)	32. (A)(B)(C)(D)	52. (A)(B)(C)(D)	72. (A)(B)(C)(D)
13. (A)(B)(C)(D)	33. (A)(B)(C)(D)	53. (A)(B)(C)(D)	73. (A)(B)(C)(D)
14. (A)(B)(C)(D)	34. (A)(B)(C)(D)	54. (A)(B)(C)(D)	74. (A)(B)(C)(D)
15. (A)(B)(C)(D)	35. (A)(B)(C)(D)	55. (A)(B)(C)(D)	75. (A)(B)(C)(D)
16. (A)(B)(C)(D)	36. (A)(B)(C)(D)	56. (A)(B)(C)(D)	76. (A)(B)(C)(D)
17. (A)(B)(C)(D)	37. (A)(B)(C)(D)	57. (A)(B)(C)(D)	77. (A)(B)(C)(D)
18. (A)(B)(C)(D)	38. (A)(B)(C)(D)	58. (A)(B)(C)(D)	78. (A)(B)(C)(D)
19. (A)(B)(C)(D)	39. (A)(B)(C)(D)	59. (A)(B)(C)(D)	79. (A)(B)(C)(D)
20. (A)(B)(C)(D)	40. (A)(B)(C)(D)	60. (A)(B)(C)(D)	80. (A)(B)(C)(D)

Answer Sheet – Mathematics

1. (A) (B) (C) (D)
2. (A) (B) (C) (D)
3. (A) (B) (C) (D)
4. (A) (B) (C) (D)
5. (A) (B) (C) (D)
6. (A) (B) (C) (D)
7. (A) (B) (C) (D)
8. (A) (B) (C) (D)
9. (A) (B) (C) (D)
10. (A) (B) (C) (D)
11. (A) (B) (C) (D)
12. (A) (B) (C) (D)
13. (A) (B) (C) (D)
14. (A) (B) (C) (D)
15. (A) (B) (C) (D)
16. (A) (B) (C) (D)
17. (A) (B) (C) (D)
18. (A) (B) (C) (D)
19. (A) (B) (C) (D)
20. (A) (B) (C) (D)
21. (A) (B) (C) (D)
22. (A) (B) (C) (D)
23. (A) (B) (C) (D)
24. (A) (B) (C) (D)
25. (A) (B) (C) (D)
26. (A) (B) (C) (D)
27. (A) (B) (C) (D)
28. (A) (B) (C) (D)
29. (A) (B) (C) (D)
30. (A) (B) (C) (D)
31. (A) (B) (C) (D)
32. (A) (B) (C) (D)
33. (A) (B) (C) (D)
34. (A) (B) (C) (D)
35. (A) (B) (C) (D)
36. (A) (B) (C) (D)
37. (A) (B) (C) (D)
38. (A) (B) (C) (D)
39. (A) (B) (C) (D)
40. (A) (B) (C) (D)
41. (A) (B) (C) (D)
42. (A) (B) (C) (D)
43. (A) (B) (C) (D)
44. (A) (B) (C) (D)
45. (A) (B) (C) (D)
46. (A) (B) (C) (D)
47. (A) (B) (C) (D)
48. (A) (B) (C) (D)
49. (A) (B) (C) (D)
50. (A) (B) (C) (D)

Answer Sheet – Science

1. A B C D
2. A B C D
3. A B C D
4. A B C D
5. A B C D
6. A B C D
7. A B C D
8. A B C D
9. A B C D
10. A B C D
11. A B C D
12. A B C D
13. A B C D
14. A B C D
15. A B C D
16. A B C D
17. A B C D
18. A B C D
19. A B C D
20. A B C D
21. A B C D
22. A B C D
23. A B C D
24. A B C D
25. A B C D
26. A B C D
27. A B C D
28. A B C D
29. A B C D
30. A B C D
31. A B C D
32. A B C D
33. A B C D
34. A B C D
35. A B C D
36. A B C D
37. A B C D
38. A B C D
39. A B C D
40. A B C D
41. A B C D
42. A B C D
43. A B C D
44. A B C D
45. A B C D
46. A B C D
47. A B C D
48. A B C D
49. A B C D
50. A B C D
51. A B C D
52. A B C D
53. A B C D
54. A B C D
55. A B C D
56. A B C D
57. A B C D
58. A B C D
59. A B C D
60. A B C D
61. A B C D
62. A B C D
63. A B C D
64. A B C D
65. A B C D
66. A B C D
67. A B C D
68. A B C D
69. A B C D
70. A B C D
71. A B C D
72. A B C D
73. A B C D
74. A B C D
75. A B C D

Section I - Verbal Ability

Directions: The following questions are based on several reading passages. Each passage is followed by a series of questions. Read each passage carefully, and then answer the questions based on it. You may reread the passage as often as you wish. When you have finished answering the questions based on one passage, go right onto the next passage. Choose the best answer based on the information given and implied.

Questions 1 - 4 refer to the following passage.

Passage 1 - The Crusades

In 1095 Pope Urban II proclaimed the First Crusade with the intent and stated goal to restore Christian access to holy places in and around Jerusalem. Over the next 200 years there were 6 major crusades and numerous minor crusades in the fight for control of the "Holy Land." Historians are divided on the real purpose of the Crusades, some believing that it was part of a purely defensive war against Islamic conquest; some see them as part of a long-running conflict at the frontiers of Europe; and others see them as confident, aggressive, papal-led expansion attempts by Western Christendom. The impact of the crusades was profound, and judgment of the Crusaders ranges from laudatory to highly critical. However, all agree that the Crusades and wars waged during those crusades were brutal and often bloody. Several hundred thousand Roman Catholic Christians joined the Crusades, they were Christians from all over Europe.

Europe at the time was under the Feudal System, so while the Crusaders made vows to the Church, they also were beholden to their Feudal Lords. This led to the Crusaders not only fighting the Saracen, the commonly used word for Muslim at the time, but also each other for power and economic gain in the Holy Land. This infighting between the Crusaders is why many historians hold the view that the Crusades were simply a front for Europe to invade the Holy Land for economic gain in the name of the Church. Another factor contributing to this theory is that while the army of crusaders marched towards Jerusalem they pillaged the land as they went. The church and feudal Lords vowing to return the land to its original beauty, and inhabitants, this rarely happened though, as the Lords often kept the land for themselves. A full 800 years after the Crusades, Pope John Paul II expressed his sorrow for the massacre of innocent people and the lasting damage that the Medieval church caused in that area of the World.

1. What is the tone of this article?

a. Subjective
b. Objective
c. Persuasive
d. None of the Above

2. What can all historians agree on concerning the Crusades?

a. It achieved great things
b. It stabilized the Holy Land
c. It was bloody and brutal
d. It helped defend Europe from the Byzantine Empire

3. What impact did the feudal system have on the Crusades?

a. It unified the Crusaders
b. It helped gather volunteers
c. It had no effect on the Crusades
d. It led to infighting, causing more damage than good

4. What does Saracen mean?

a. Muslim
b. Christian
c. Knight
d. Holy Land

Questions 5 - 8 refer to the following passage.

ABC Electric Warranty

ABC Electric Company warrants that its products are free from defects in material and workmanship. Subject to the conditions and limitations set forth below, ABC Electric will, at its option, either repair or replace any part of its products that prove defective due to improper workmanship or materials.

This limited warranty does not cover any damage to the product from improper installation, accident, abuse, misuse, natural disaster, insufficient or excessive electrical supply, abnormal mechanical or environmental conditions, or any unauthorized disassembly, repair, or modification.

This limited warranty also does not apply to any product on which the original identification information has been altered, or removed, has not been handled or packaged correctly, or has been sold as second-hand.

This limited warranty covers only repair, replacement, refund or credit for defective ABC Electric products, as provided above.

5. I tried to repair my ABC Electric blender, but could not, so can I get it repaired under this warranty?

a. Yes, the warranty still covers the blender
b. No, the warranty does not cover the blender
c. Uncertain. ABC Electric may or may not cover re-

pairs under this warranty

6. My ABC Electric fan is not working. Will ABC Electric provide a new one or repair this one?

a. ABC Electric will repair my fan
b. ABC Electric will replace my fan
c. ABC Electric could either replace or repair my fan can request either a replacement or a repair.

7. My stove was damaged in a flood. Does this warranty cover my stove?

a. Yes, it is covered.
b. No, it is not covered.
c. It may or may not be covered.
d. ABC Electric will decide if it is covered

8. Which of the following is an example of improper workmanship?

a. Missing parts
b. Defective parts
c. Scratches on the front
d. None of the above

Questions 9 – 12 refer to the following passage.

Passage 2 - Women and Advertising

Only in the last few generations have media messages been so widespread and so readily seen, heard, and read by so many people. Advertising is an important part of both selling and buying anything from soap to cereal to jeans. For whatever reason, more consumers are women than are men. Media message are subtle but powerful, and more attention has been paid lately to how these message affect women. Of all the products that women buy, makeup, clothes, and other stylistic or cosmetic products are among the most popular. This means that companies focus their advertising on women, promising them that their product will make her feel, look, or smell better than the next company's product will. This competition has resulted in advertising that is more and more ideal and less and less possible for everyday women. However, because women do look to these ideals and the products they represent as how they can potentially become, many women have developed unhealthy attitudes about themselves when they have failed to become those ideals.

In recent years, more companies have tried to change advertisements to be healthier for women. This includes featuring models of more sizes and addressing a huge outcry against unfair tools such as airbrushing and photo editing. There is debate about what the right balance between real and ideal is, because fashion is also considered art and some changes are made to purposefully elevate fashionable products and signify that they are creative, innovative, and the work of individual people. Artists want their freedom protected as much as women do, and advertising agencies are often caught in the middle.

Some claim that the companies who make these changes are not doing enough. Many people worry that there are still not enough models of different sizes and different ethnicities. Some people claim that companies use this healthier type of advertisement not for the good of women, but because they would like to sell products to the women who are looking for these kinds of messages. This is also a hard balance to find: companies need to make money, and women need to feel respected.
While the focus of this change has been on women, advertising can also affect men, and this change will hopefully be a lesson on media for all consumers.

9. The second paragraph states that advertising focuses on women

a. to shape what the ideal should be

b. because women buy makeup

c. because women are easily persuaded

d. because of the types of products that women buy

10. According to the passage, fashion artists and female consumers are at odds because

a. there is a debate going on and disagreement drives people apart

b. both of them are trying to protect their freedom to do something

c. artists want to elevate their products above the reach of women

d. women are creative, innovative, individual people

11. The author uses the phrase "for whatever reason" in this passage to

a. keep the focus of the paragraph on media messages and not on the differences between men and women

b. show that the reason for this is unimportant

c. argue that it is stupid that more women are consumers than men

d. show that he or she is tired of talking about why media messages are important

12. This passage suggests that

a. advertising companies are still working on making their messages better

b. all advertising companies seek to be more approachable for women

c. women are only buying from companies that respect them

d. artists could stop producing fashionable products if they feel bullied

Questions 13 - 16 refer to the following passage.

FDR, the Treaty of Versailles, and the Fourteen Points

At the conclusion of World War I, those who had won the war and those who were forced to admit defeat welcomed the end of the war and expected that a peace treaty would be signed. The American president, Franklin D. Roosevelt, played an important part in proposing what the agreements should be and did so through his Fourteen Points.
World War I had begun in 1914 when an Austrian archduke was assassinated, leading to a domino effect that pulled the world's most powerful countries into war on a large scale. The war catalysed the creation and use of deadly weapons that had not previously existed, resulting in a great loss of soldiers on both sides of the fighting. More than 9 million soldiers were killed.

The United States agreed to enter the war right before it ended, and many believed that its decision to become finally involved brought on the end of the war. FDR made it very clear that the U.S. was entering the war for moral reasons and had an agenda focused on world peace. The Fourteen Points were individual goals and ideas (focused on peace, free trade, open communication, and self-reliance) that FDR wanted the power nations to strive for now that the war had ended. He was optimistic and had many ideas about what could be accomplished through, and during the post-war peace. However, FDR's fourteen points were poorly received when he presented them to the leaders of other world powers, many of whom wanted only to help their own countries and to punish the Germans for fueling the war, and they fell by the wayside. World War II was imminent, for Germany lost everything.

Some historians believe that the other leaders who participated in the Treaty of Versailles weren't receptive to the Fourteen Points because World War I was fought almost entirely on European soil, and the United States lost much less than did the other powers. FDR was in a unique position to determine the fate of the war, but doing it on his own terms did not help accomplish his goals. This is only one historical example of how the United State has tried to use its power as an important country, but found itself limited because of geological or ideological factors.

13. The main idea of this passage is that

a. World War I was unfair because no fighting took place in America

b. World War II happened because of the Treaty of Versailles

c. the power the United States has to help other countries also prevents it from helping other countries

d. Franklin D. Roosevelt was one of the United States' smartest presidents

14. According to the second paragraph, World War I started because

a. an archduke was assassinated

b. weapons that were more deadly had been developed

c. a domino effect of allies agreeing to help each other

d. the world's most powerful countries were large

15. The author includes the detail that 9 million soldiers were killed

a. to demonstrate why European leaders were hesitant to accept peace

b. to show the reader the dangers of deadly weapons

c. to make the reader think about which countries lost the most soldiers

d. to demonstrate why World War II was imminent

16. According to this passage, catalysed means

a. analyzed
b. sped up
c. invented
d. funded

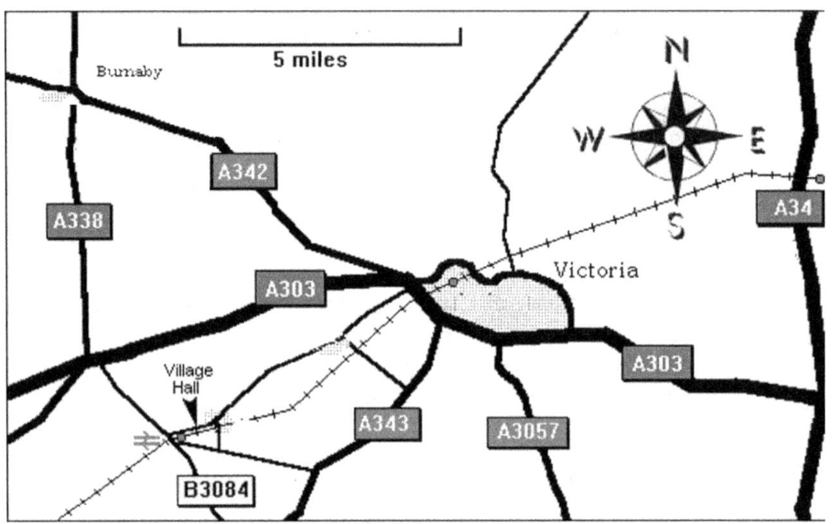

17. Approximately how far is Victoria to Burnaby?

a. About 10 miles
b. About 5 miles
c. About 15 miles
d. About 20 miles

18. How is the Village Hall from Victoria?

a. About 10 miles
b. About 5 miles
c. About 15 miles
d. About 20 miles

Questions 19 - 22 refer to the following passage.

Chocolate Chip Cookies

3/4 cup sugar
3/4 cup packed brown sugar
1 cup butter, softened
2 large eggs, beaten
1 teaspoon vanilla extract
2 1/4 cups all-purpose flour
1 teaspoon baking soda
3/4 teaspoon salt
2 cups semisweet chocolate chips
If desired, 1 cup chopped pecans, or chopped walnuts.
Preheat oven to 375 degrees.

Mix sugar, brown sugar, butter, vanilla and eggs in a large bowl. Stir in flour, baking soda, and salt. The dough will be very stiff.

Stir in chocolate chips by hand with a sturdy wooden spoon. Add the pecans, or other nuts, if desired. Stir until the chocolate chips and nuts are evenly dispersed.

Drop dough by rounded tablespoonfuls 2 inches apart onto a cookie sheet.

Bake 8 to 10 minutes, or, until light brown. Cookies may look underdone, but they will finish cooking after you take them out of the oven.

19. What is the correct order for adding these ingredients?

a. Brown sugar, baking soda, chocolate chips
b. Baking soda, brown sugar, chocolate chips
c. Chocolate chips, baking soda, brown sugar
d. Baking soda, chocolate chips, brown sugar

20. What does sturdy mean?

a. Long
b. Strong
c. Short
d. Wide

21. What does disperse mean?

a. Scatter
b. To form a ball
c. To stir
d. To beat

22. When can you stop stirring the nuts?

a. When the cookies are cooked.
b. When the nuts are evenly distributed.
c. When the nuts are added.
d. After the chocolate chips are added.

Questions 23 - 26 refer to the following passage.

Passage 5 -Winged Victory of Samothrace: the Statue of the Gods

Students who read about the "Winged Victory of Samothrace" probably won't be able to visualize the statue. However, almost anyone who knows a little about statues will recognize it when they see it: it is the statue of a winged woman who does not have arms or a head. Even the most famous pieces of art may be recognized by sight but not by name.

This iconic statue is of the Greek goddess Nike, who represented victory and was called Victoria by the Romans. The statue is sometimes called the "Nike of Samothrace." She was often displayed in Greek art as driving a chariot, and her speed or efficiency with the chariot may be what her wings symbolize. It is said that the statue was created around 200 BCE to celebrate a battle that was won at sea. Archaeologists and art historians believe the statue originally may have been part of a temple or other building, even one of the most important temples, Megaloi Theoi, just as many statues were used during that time.

"Winged Victory" does indeed appear to have had arms and a head when it was originally created, and it is unclear why they were removed or lost. Indeed, they have never been discovered, even with all the excavation that has taken place. Many speculate that one of her arms was raised and put to her mouth, as though she was shouting or calling out, which is consistent with the idea of her as a war figure. If the missing pieces were ever to be found, they might give Greek and art historians more of an idea of what Nike represented or how the statue was used. Learning about pieces of art through details like these can help students remember time frames or locations, as well as learn about the people who occupied them.

23. Why does the title says the statue is "of the Gods?"

a. the statue is very beautiful and even a god would find it beautiful

b. the statue is of a Greek goddess, and gods were of primary importance to the Greek

c. Nike lead the gods into war

d. the statues were used at the temple of the gods and so it belonged to them

24. The third paragraph states that

a. the statue is related to war and was probably broken apart by foreign soldiers

b. the arms and head of the statue cannot be found because all the excavation has taken place

c. speculations have been made about what the entire statue looked like and what it symbolized

d. the statue has no arms or head because the sculptor lost them

25. The author's main purpose in writing this passage is to

a. demonstrate that art and culture are related and one can teach us about the other

b. persuade readers to become archaeologists and find the missing pieces of the statue

c. teach readers about the Greek goddess Nike

d. to teach readers the name of a statue they probably recognize

26. The author specifies the indirect audience as "students" because

a. it is probably a student who is taking this test

b. most young people don't know much about art yet and most young people are students

c. students read more than people who are not students

d. the passage is based on a discussion of what we can learn about culture from art

Questions 27 - 30 refer to the following passage.

Lowest Price Guarantee

Get it for less. Guaranteed!

ABC Electric will beat any advertised price by 10% of the difference.

1) If you find a lower advertised price, we will beat it by 10% of the difference.

2) If you find a lower advertised price within 30 days* of your purchase we will beat it by 10% of the difference.

3) If our own price is reduced within 30 days* of your purchase, bring in your receipt and we will refund the difference.

*14 days for computers, monitors, printers, laptops, tablets, cellular & wireless devices, home security products, projectors, camcorders, digital cameras, radar detectors, portable DVD players, DJ and pro-audio equipment, and air conditioners.

27. I bought a radar detector 15 days ago and saw an ad for the same model only cheaper. Can I get 10% of the difference refunded?

a. Yes. Since it is less than 30 days, you can get 10% of the difference refunded.

b. No. Since it is more than 14 days, you cannot get 10% of the difference re-funded.

c. It depends on the cashier.

d. Yes. You can get the difference refunded.

28. I bought a flat-screen TV for $500 10 days ago and found an advertisement for the same TV, at another store, on sale for $400. How much will ABC refund under this guarantee?

a. $100

b. $110

c. $10

d. $400

29. What is the purpose of this passage?

a. To inform

b. To educate

c. To persuade

d. To entertain

Questions 30 - 33 refer to the following passage.

Passage 6 - What Is Mardi Gras?

Mardi Gras is fast becoming one of the South's most famous and most celebrated holidays. The word Mardi Gras comes from the French and the literal translation is "Fat Tuesday." The holiday has also been called Shrove Tuesday, due to its associations with Lent. The purpose of Mardi Gras is to celebrate and enjoy before the Lenten season of fasting and repentance begins.

What originated by the French Explorers in New Orleans, Louisiana in the 17th century is now celebrated all over the world. Panama, Italy, Belgium and Brazil all host large scale Mardi Gras celebrations, and many smaller cities and towns celebrate this fun loving Tuesday as well. Usually held in February or early March, Mardi Gras is a day of extravagance, a day for people to eat, drink and be merry, to wear costumes, masks and to dance to jazz music.
The French explorers on the Mississippi River would be in shock today if they saw the opulence of the parades and floats that grace the New Orleans streets during Mardi Gras these days. Parades in New Orleans are divided by organizations. These are more commonly known as Krewes.

Being a member of a Krewe is quite a task because Krewes are responsible for overseeing the parades. Each Krewe's parade is ruled by a Mardi Gras "King and Queen." The role of the King and Queen is to "bestow" gifts on their adoring fans as the floats ride along the street. They throw doubloons, which is fake money and usually colored green, purple and gold, which are the colors of Mardi Gras. Beads in those color shades are also thrown and cups are thrown as well. Beads are by far the most popular souvenir of any Mardi Gras parade, with each spectator attempting to gather as many as possible.

30. The purpose of Mardi Gras is to

a. Repent for a month.
b. Celebrate in extravagant ways.
c. Be a member of a Krewe.
d. Explore the Mississippi.

31. From reading the passage we can infer that "Kings and Queens,"

a. Have to be members of a Krewe.
b. Have to be French.
c. Have to know how to speak French.
d. Have to give away their own money.

32. Which group of people began to hold Mardi Gras celebrations?

a. Settlers from Italy
b. Members of Krewes
c. French explorers
d. Belgium explorers

33. In the context of the passage, what does spectator mean?

a. Someone who participates actively
b. Someone who watches the parade's action
c. Someone on the parade floats
d. Someone who does not celebrate Mardi Gras

Verbal Ability Part II – Vocabulary

34. Choose the adjective that means shocking, terrible or wicked.

a. Pleasantries
b. Heinous
c. Shrewd
d. Provencal

35. Choose the noun that means a person or thing that tells or announces the coming of someone or something.

a. Harbinger
b. Evasion
c. Bleak
d. Craven

36. Choose a word that means the same as the underlined word.

He wasn't especially generous. All the servings were very <u>judicious</u>.

a. Abundant
b. Careful
c. Extravagant
d. Careless

37. Fill in the blank.

Because of the growing use of ________as a fuel, corn production has greatly increased.

a. Alcohol
b. Ethanol
c. Natural gas
d. Oil

38. Fill in the blank.

In heavily industrialized areas, the pollution of the air causes many to develop ________ diseases.

a. Respiratory
b. Cardiac
c. Alimentary
d. Circulatory

39. Choose the best definition of inherent.

a. To receive money in a will
b. An essential part of
c. To receive money from a will
d. None of the above

40. Choose the best definition of vapid.

a. adj. tasteless or bland
b. v. To inflict, as a revenge or punishment
c. v. to convert into gas
d. v. to go up in smoke

41. Choose the best definition of waif.

a. n. a sick and hungry child
b. n. an orphan staying in a foster home
c. n. homeless child or stray
d. n. a type of French bread eaten with cheese

42. Choose the adjective that means similar or identical.

a. Soluble
b. Assembly
c. Conclave
d. Homologous

43. Choose a word with the same meaning as the underlined word.

We used that operating system 20 years ago, now it is obsolete.

a. Functional
b. Disused
c. Obese
d. None of the Above

44. Choose the word with the same meaning as the underlined word

His bad manners really rankle me.

a. Annoy
b. Obsolete
c. Enliven
d. None of the above

45. Fill in the blank.

Because hydroelectric power is a _________ source of energy, its use is excellent for the environment.

a. Significant
b. Disposable
c. Renewable
d. Reusable

46. Choose the best definition of torpid.

a. Fast
b. Rapid
c. Sluggish
d. Violent

47. Choose the best definition of gregarious.

a. Sociable
b. Introverted
c. Large
d. Solitary

48. Choose the best definition of mutation.

a. v. To utter with a loud and vehement voice
b. n. change or alteration
c. n. An act or exercise of will
d. v. To cause to be one

49. Choose the best definition of lithe.

a. adj. small in size
b. adj. Artificial
c. adj. flexible or plaint
d. adj. fake

50. Choose the best definition of resent.

a. adj. To express displeasure or indignation
b. v. To cause to be one
c. adj. Clumsy
d. adj. strong feelings of love

51. Choose the adjective that means irrelevant not having substance or matter.

a. Immaterial
b. Prohibition
c. Prediction
d. Brokerage

52. Choose the adjective that means perfect, no faults or errors.

a. Impeccable
b. Formidable
c. Genteel
d. Disputation

53. Choose the best definition of pudgy.

a. v. to draw general inferences
b. Adj. fat, plump and overweight
c. n. permanence
d. adj. spoilt or bad condition

54. Choose the best definition of alloy.

a. To mix with something superior
b. To mix
c. To mix with something inferior
d. To purify

55. Fill in the blank.

The process required the use of highly _________ liquids, so fire extinguishers were everywhere in the factory.

a. Erratic
b. Combustible
c. Stable
d. Neutral

56. Choose the best definition for the underlined word.

We don't want to hear the whole thing. Just the salient facts please.

a. Irrelevant
b. Erroneous
c. Relevant
d. Trivial

57. Choose the best definition for the underlined word.

I don't know why he is being so nice. I am sure he has an ulterior motive.

a. Inferior
b. Additional
c. Simplistic
d. Unfortunate

58. Choose the noun that means ruling council of a military government.

a. Retribution
b. Counsel
c. Virago
d. Junta

59. Choose a noun that means someone who takes more time than necessary.

a. Manager
b. Haggard
c. Laggard
d. Expound

60. Choose an adjective that means lacking enthusiasm, strength or energy.

a. Hapless
b. Languid
c. Ubiquitous
d. Promiscuous

Section II – Math

1. It is known that $x^2 + 4x = 5$. Then x can be

a. 0
b. -5
c. 1
d. Either (b) or (c)

2. (a + b)2 = 4ab. What is necessarily correct?

a. a > b
b. a < b
c. a = b
d. None of the Above

3. The sum of the digits of a 2-digit number is 12. If we switch the digits, the resulting number will be greater than the initial one by 36. Find the initial number.

a. 39
b. 48
c. 57
d. 75

4. In a class of 83 students, 72 are present. What percent of student is absent?

a. 12
b. 13
c. 14
d. 15

5. Kate's father is 32 years older than Kate is. In 5 years, he will be five times older. How old is Kate?

a. 2
b. 3
c. 5
d. 6

6. If Lynn can type a page in p minutes, what portion of the page can she do in 5 minutes?

a. 5/p
b. p - 5
c. p + 5
d. p/5

7. Find the mean of these set of numbers – 2.5, 10.2, 4.5, 1.25, 7.05, 20.8

a. 7.6
b. 45.6
c. 7
d. 1.25

8. If Sally can paint a house in 4 hours, and John can paint the same house in 6 hours, how long will it take for both of them to paint the house together?

a. 2 hours and 24 minutes
b. 3 hours and 12 minutes
c. 3 hours and 44 minutes
d. 4 hours and 10 minutes

9. A bullet weighing 350g is shot towards a target at a velocity of 250m/s. Calculate the momentum of the bullet?

a. 1.4 kg x m/s towards target
b. 87.5 kg x m/s towards target
c. 87500 kg x m/s towards target
d. 8.75 kg x m/s towards target

10. Using the quadratic formula, solve the quadratic equation: $x^2 - 9x + 14 = 0$

a. 2 and 7
b. -2 and 7
c. -7 and -2
d. -7 and 2

11. Employees of a discount appliance store receive an additional 20% off the lowest price on any item. If an employee purchases a dishwasher during a 15% off sale, how much will he pay if the dishwasher originally cost $450?

a. $280.90
b. $287.00
c. $292.50
d. $306.00

12. The sale price of a car is $12,590, which is 20% off the original price. What is the original price?

a. $14,310.40
b. $14,990.90
c. $15,108.00
d. $15,737.50

13. A goat eats 214 kg. of hay in 60 days, while a cow eats the same amount in 15 days. How long will it take them to eat this hay together?

a. 37.5
b. 75
c. 12
d. 15

14. Express 125% as a decimal.

a. .125
b. 12.5
c. 1.25
d. 125

15. What are the prime factors of 125?

a. 5 x 25
b. 5 x 5 x 5
d. All of the above
d. None of the above

16. Solve for x: 30 is 40% of x

a. 60
b. 90
c. 85
d. 75

17. Which of these object has greater momentum, a 2kg truck moving east at 3.5m/s or a 4.3kg truck moving south at 1.5m/s?

a. The first truck at 7 kg x m/s moving east
b. The second truck at 7.45 kg x m/s due south
c. The first truck at 6.45 kg x m/s due east

d. The second truck at 7 kg x m/s due south

18. 12 ½% of x is equal to 50.
Solve for x.

a. 300
b. 400
c. 450
d. 350

19. Express 24/56 as a reduced common fraction.

a. 4/9
b. 4/11
c. 3/7
d. 3/8

20. What are the prime factors of 132?

a. 4 x 3 x 11
b. 2 x 2 x 2 x 3 x 11
c. 2 x 6 x 11
d. 2 x 2 x 3 x 11

21. Express 87% as a decimal.

a. .087
b. 8.7
c. .87
d. 87

22. 60 is 75% of x. Solve for x.

a. 80
b. 90
c. 75
d. 70

23. Find the median of these set of test scores taken from a class of students – 90, 80, 77, 86, 50, 91, 73, 66, 69, 45, 43, 65, 75

a. 13
b. 73
c. 9
d. 706

24. 4.7 + .9 + .01 =

a. 5.5
b. 6.51
c. 5.61
d. 5.7

25. .87 - .48 =

a. .39
b. .49
c. .41
d. .37

26. The physician ordered 100 mg Ibuprofen/kg of body weight; on hand is 230 mg/tablet. The child weighs 50 lb. How many tablets will you give?

a. 10 tablets
b. 5 tablets
c. 1 tablet
d. 12 tablets

27. Find the mode from these numbers: 7,2,3,9,6,5,1,4,8

a. 1
b. 5
c. 9
d. None of the above

28. Simplify 4^3

a. 20
b. 32
c. 64
d. 108

29. The physician ordered 5 mL of Capacitate; 15 mL/tsp is on hand. How many teaspoons will you give?

a. 0.05 tsp
b. 0.03 tsp
c. 0.5 tsp
d. 0.3 tsp

30. Using the quadratic formula, solve the quadratic equation: $x - 31/x = 0$

a. $-\sqrt{13}$ and $\sqrt{13}$
b. $-\sqrt{31}$ and $\sqrt{31}$
c. $-\sqrt{31}$ and $2\sqrt{31}$
d. $-\sqrt{3}$ and $\sqrt{3}$

31. The manager of a weaving factory estimates that if 10 machines run on 100% efficiency for 8 hours, they will produce 1450 meters of cloth. However, due to some technical problems, 4 machines run of 95% efficiency and the remaining 6 at 90% efficiency. How many meters of cloth can these machines will produce in 8 hours?

a. 1334 meters
b. 1310 meters
c. 1300 meters
d. 1285 meters

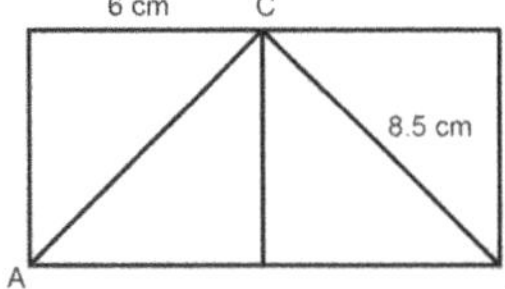

Note: figure not drawn to scale

32. Assuming the 2 quadrangles in the figure are identical rectangles, what is the perimeter of △ABC in the above shape?

a. 25.5 cm
b. 27 cm
c. 30 cm
d. 29 cm

33. Solve for x if, $10^2 \times 100^2 = 1000^x$

a. x = 2
b. x = 3
c. x = -2
d. x = 0

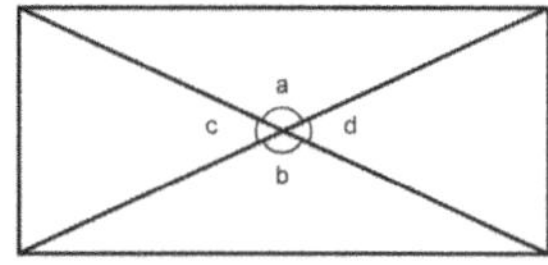

34. What is the sum of angles a, b, c and d in the rectangle above?

a. 180°
b. 360°
c. 90°
d. 120°

35. Find the mode from these test results: 2, 4, 2, 6, 4, 9, 6, 7, 2, 9, 7, 6, 4, 10, 10, 2, 6, 7, 9

a. 2 and 9
b. 2
c. 2 and 6
d. 2 and 7

36. Convert from scientific notation: 5.63×10^6

a. 5,630,000
b. 563,000
c. 5630
d. 0.000005.630

37. 30 mg is the same mass as:

a. 0.0003 kg.
b. 0.03 grams
c. 300 decigrams
d. 0.3 grams

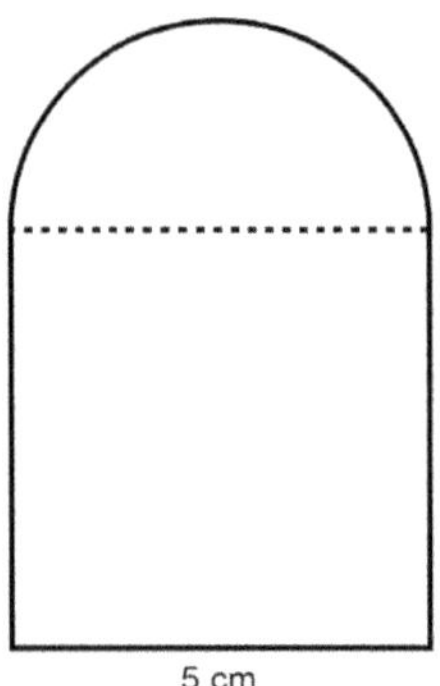

Note: figure not drawn to scale

38. What is the perimeter of the above shape?

a. 17.5 π cm
b. 20 π cm
c. 15 π cm
d. 25 π cm

39. 0.101 mm. =

a. .0101 cm
b. 1.01 cm
c. 0.00101 cm
d. 10.10 cm

40. Using the factoring method, solve the quadratic equation: $2x^2 - 3x = 0$

a. 0 and 1.5
b. 1.5 and 2
c. 2 and 2.5
d. 0 and 2

41. How much water can be stored in a cylindrical container 5 meters in diameter and 12 meters high?

a. 223.65 m^3
b. 235.65 m^3
c. 240.65 m^3
d. 252.65 m^3

42. Convert 0.045 to scientific notation.

a. 4.5×10^{-2}
b. 4.5×10^{2}
c. 4.05×10^{-2}
d. 4.5×10^{-3}

43.

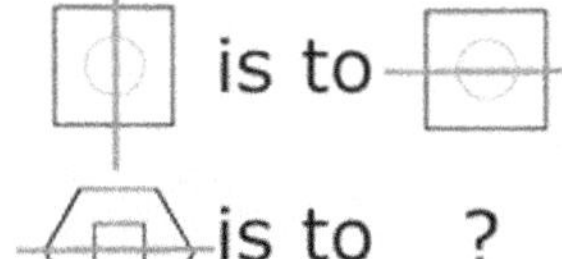

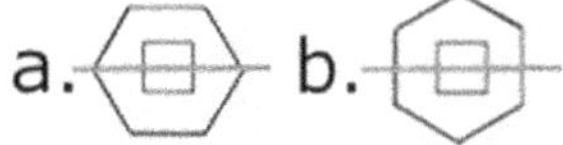

c. d.

44.

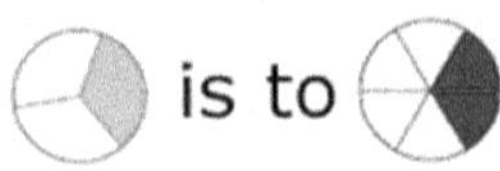

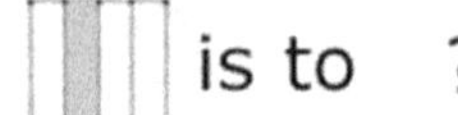

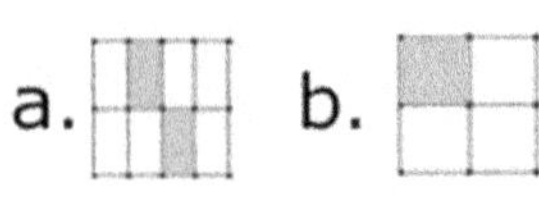

c. d.

45.

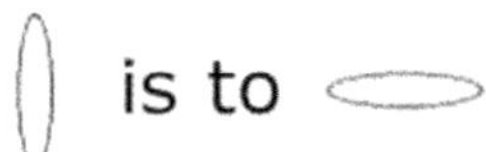

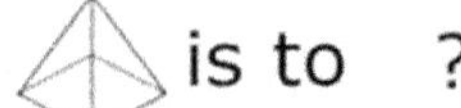

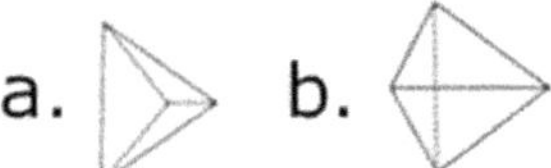

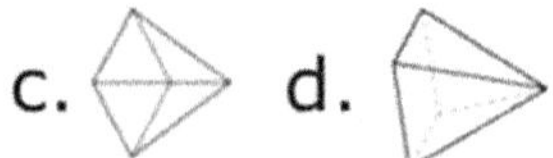

46.

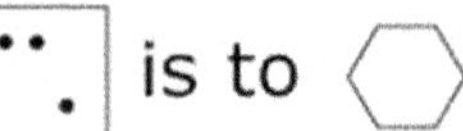

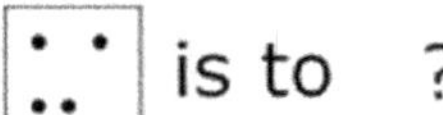

a. b.

c. d.

47. Factor the polynomial $9x^2 - 6x + 12$.

a. $3(x^2 - 2x + 9)$

b. $3(3x^2 - 3x + 4)$

c. $9(x^2 - 3x + 3)$

d. $3(3x^2 - 2x + 4)$

48. 389 + 454 =

a. 853

b. 833

c. 843

d. 863

49. 9,177 + 7,204 =

a. 16,4712

b. 16,371

c. 16,381

d. 15,412

50. 2,199 + 5,832 =

a. 8,331

b. 8,041

c. 8,141

d. 8,031

Section III – Science

1. A soccer ball is kicked and travels at a velocity of 12 m/sec. After 60 seconds, it comes to a stop. What is the acceleration?

a. -0.2 m/sec^2
b. 0.2 m/sec^2
c. 1 m/sec^2
d. 0.5 m/sec^2

2. A molecule of water contains hydrogen and oxygen in a 1:8 ratio by mass. This is a statement of

a. The law of multiple proportions
b. The law of conservation of mass
c. The law of conservation of energy
d. The law of constant composition

3. Electrons play a critical role in

a. Electricity
b. Magnetism
c. Thermal conductivity
d. All of the above

4. An idea concerning a phenomena and possible explanations for that phenomena is a/an

a. Theory.
b. Experiment.
c. Inference.
d. Hypothesis.

5. Define chromosomes.

a. Structures in a cell nucleus that carry genetic material.

b. Consist of thousands of DNA strands.

c. Total 46 in a normal human cell.

d. All of the above

6. A base is

a. A compound that reacts with an acid to form a salt.

b. A molecule or ion that captures hydrogen ions.

c. A molecule or ion that donates an electron pair to form a chemical bond.

d. All of the above are true

7. Which disease of the circulatory system is one of the most frequent causes of death in North America?

a. The cold

b. Pneumonia

c. Arthritis

d. Heart disease

8. How fast can a person walk if they travel 1000 m in 20 minutes?

a. 25 meters

b. 50 meters

c. 100 meters

d. None of the above

9. A substance containing atoms of more than one element in a definite ratio is called a(n)

a. Compound.
b. Element.
c. Mixture.
d. Molecule.

10. Which of the following describes a plasma membrane?

a. Lipids with embedded proteins
b. An outer lipid layer and an inner lipid layer
c. Proteins embedded in lipid bilayer
d. Altering protein and lipid layers

11. Protein biosynthesis is defined as

a. The addition of protein to foods that lack it.
b. Ribosomes synthesizing proteins in the endoplasmic reticulum.
c. The process of proteasomes degrading cytoplasm.
d. Proteins "flowing" through the ER into the plasma membrane.

12. When we speak of separating organelles through centrifugation, we're speaking of

a. Cell fractionation
b. Flow cytometry
c. Immunoprecipation
d. Detergents

13. What is the difference between Strong Nuclear Force and Weak Nuclear Force?

a. The Strong Nuclear Force is an attractive force that binds protons and neutrons and maintains the structure of the nucleus, and the Weak Nuclear Force is responsible for the radioactive beta decay and other subatomic reactions.

b. The Strong Nuclear Force is responsible for the radioactive beta decay and other subatomic reactions, and the Weak Nuclear Force is an attractive force that binds protons and neutrons and maintains the structure of the nucleus.

c. The Weak Nuclear Force is feeble and the Strong Nuclear Force is robust.

d. The Strong Nuclear Force is a negative force that releases protons and neutrons and threatens the structure of the nucleus, and the Weak Nuclear Force is an attractive force that binds protons and neutrons and maintains the structure of the nucleus.

14. 1000 N force is applied to a concrete block that weights 500 pounds. How fast will this force accelerate the block?

a. 1 m/sec^2

b. 2 m/sec^2

c. 3 m/sec^2

d. 5 m/sec^2

15. What type of research deals with the quality, type or components of a group, substance, or mixture.

a. Quantitative

b. Dependent

c. Scientific

d. Qualitative

16. When a measurement is recorded, it includes the _________ ________, which are all the digits that are certain plus one uncertain digit.

a. Major figures

b. Significant figures

c. Relative figures

d. Relevant figures

17. The equation $E = mc^2$ is based on the ______________________, and states that ______equals _____ times the _____________^{2}.

a. The equation $E = mc^2$ is based on the 2nd Law of Thermodynamics, and states that Mass equals Energy times (the Velocity of light)^2.

b. The equation $E = mc^2$ is based on the Law of Conservation of Mass and Energy, and states that Energy equals Mass times (the Velocity of light)^2.

c. The equation $E = mc^2$ is based on the 1st Law of Thermodynamics, and states that Mass equals Energy times (the Velocity of sound)^2.

d. The equation $E = mc^2$ is based on the Law of Conservation of Mass and Energy, and states that the Velocity of light equals Energy times (the Mass)^2.

18. Describe a pH indicator.

a. A pH indicator measures hydrogen ions in a solution and show pH on a color scale.

b. A pH indicator measures oxygen ions in a solution and show pH on a color scale.

c. A pH indicator many different types of ions in a solution and shows pH on a color scale

d. None of the above

19. All acids turn blue litmus paper

a. Blue
b. Red
c. Green
d. White

20. What type of bonds involve a complete sharing of electrons and occurs most commonly between atoms that have partially filled outer shells or energy levels?

a. Covalent
b. Ionic
c. Hydrogen
d. Proportional

21. What can accept a hydrogen ion and can react with fats to form soap?

a. Acid
b. Salt
c. Base
d. Foundation

22. Which, if any, of the following statements are true?

a. Water boils at about 100 °C (212 °F) at standard atmospheric pressure.

b. The boiling point is the temperature at which the vapor pressure is higher than the atmospheric pressure around the water.

c. Water boils at a higher temperature in areas of lower pressure.

d. All of the above statements are true.

23. Which gene, whose presence as a single copy, controls the expression of a trait?

a. Principal gene
b. Latent gene
c. Recessive gene
d. Dominant gene

24. What is the mathematical function that gives the amplitude of a wave as a function of position (and sometimes, as a function of time and/or electron spin)?

a. Wavelength
b. Frequency
c. Wavenumber
d. Wavefunction

25. Which of the following is not a habitat where bacteria commonly grow?

a. Soil
b. The vacuum of space
c. Radioactive waste
d. Deep in the earth's crust

26. Within taxonomy, plants and animals are considered two basic

a. Families
b. Kingdoms
c. Domains
d. Genus

27. How much force is needed to accelerate a car that weights 200 kg to 5 m/s^2?

a. 2000 N

b. 4000 N

c. 6000 N

d. 8000 N

28. What is a chemical involved in, but not changed by, a chemical reaction by which chemical bonds are weakened and reactions accelerated.

a. A propellant

b. A reagent

c. A catalyst

d. None of the above

29. Organisms grouped into the _________ Kingdom include all unicellular organisms lacking a definite cellular arrangement such as _________ and _________.

a. Fungi, bacteria, algae

b. Protista, bacteria, amphibian

c. Protista, bacteria, algae

d. Plantae, bacteria, algae

30. Which of these statements about metals are true?

a. A metal is a substance that conducts heat and electricity.

b. A metal is shiny and reflects many colors of light, and can be hammered into sheets or drawn into wire.

c. All these statements are true.

d. About 80% of the known chemical elements are metals.

31. What type of bond does a reaction of elements with low electronegativity (almost empty outer shells) with elements with high electronegativity (mostly full outer shells) create?

a. Hydrogen
b. Covalent
c. Ionic
d. Nuclear

32. Which of the following is not an infectious bacterial disease?

a. Cholera
b. Anthrax
c. Leprosy
d. AIDS

33. Define a biological class.

a. A collection of similar or like living entities.
b. Two or more animals in a group, all having the same parent.
c. All animals sharing the same living environment.
d. All plant life that share the same physical properties.

34. Which, if any, of the following statements about prokaryotic cells is false?

a. Prokaryotic cells include such organisms as E. coli and Streptococcus.
b. Prokaryotic cells lack internal membranes and organelles.
c. Prokaryotic cells break down food using cellular respiration and fermentation.
d. All of these statements are true.

35. 1000 N force is applied to a concrete block that weights 500 pounds. How fast will this force accelerate the block?

a. -2 m/sec^2
b. 2 m/sec^2
c. 4 m/sec^2
d. 5 m/sec^2

36. What is the process of converting observed phenomena into data is called?

a. Calculation
b. Measurement
c. Valuation
d. Estimation

37. What law states that when two elements combine with to form more than one compound, the weights of one element that combine with a fixed weight of the other are in a ratio of small whole numbers?

a. The Law of Multiple Proportions
b. The Law of Definite Proportions
c. The Law of the Conservation of Energy
d. The Law of Averages

38. What word describes the wide diversity of sizes and shapes found in bacteria?

a. Morphologies
b. Cosmologies
c. Proteins
d. Spirilla

39. The mass number of an atom is

a. The total number of particles that make it up.

b. The total weight of an atom.

c. The total mass of an atom.

d. None of the above.

40. Which of these statements about mechanical energy is/are true?

a. Mechanical energy is the energy an object possesses due to its motion or due to its position.

b. Mechanical energy can be either kinetic energy (energy of motion) or potential energy (stored energy of position).

c. Objects have mechanical energy if they are in motion.

d. All of the above.

41. What three processes are involved in cell division of Eukaryotic cells?

a. Meiosis, mitosis, and interphase

b. Meiosis, mitosis, and interphase

c. Mitosis, kinematisis, and interphase

d. Mitosis, cytokinesis, and interphase

42. The __________ ________ of an element equals the number of protons in an atomic nucleus, and, along with the element symbol is one of two alternate ways to label an element.

a. Atomic unit

b. Atomic number

c. Atomic orbital

d. Nuclear number

43. Which of the following statements, if any, are correct?

a. pH is a measure of effective concentration of hydrogen ions in a solution, and is approximately related to the molarity of H+ by pH = - log [H+]

b. pH is a measure of effective concentration of oxygen ions in a solution, and is approximately related to the molarity of O+ by pH = - log [O+]

c. pH is a measure of effective concentration of hydrogen atoms in a solution, and is approximately related to the polarity of H+ by pH = - log [H+]

d. Acidity is a measure of effective concentration of hydrogen ions in a solution, and is approximately related to the molarity of H+ by pH = - log [H+]

44. What chain of nucleotides plays an important role in the creation of new proteins?

a. Deoxyribonucleic acid (DNA) is a chain of nucleotides that plays an important role in the creation of new proteins.

b. Ribonucleic acid (RNA) is a chain of nucleotides that plays an important role in the creation of new proteins.

c. There are no chains of nucleotides that play a role in the creation of proteins.

d. None of the above.

45. How much force is needed to accelerate a car that weights 200 kg to 5 m/s^2?

a. 40 N

b. 200 N

c. 1000 N

d. 1500 N

46. What law states that every chemical compound contains fixed and constant proportions (by weight) of its constituent elements?

a. The Law of Multiple Proportions
b. The Law of the Preservation of Matter
c. The Law of the Conservation of Energy
d. The Law of Definite Proportions

47. Four factors that affect rates of reaction are

a. Barometric pressure, particle size, concentration, and the presence of a facilitator.
b. Temperature, particle size, concentration, and the presence of a catalyst.
c. Temperature, container material, elevation, and the presence of instability.
d. Volatility, particle size, concentration, and the presence of a catalyst.

48. What is the term used for bacterial species which are spherical in shape?

a. Bacilli
b. Spirilla
c. Cocci
d. Spirochaetes

49. A practical test designed with the intention that its results will be relevant to a particular theory or set of theories is a/an ___________.

a. Experiment
b. Practicum
c. Theory
d. Design

50. If 3 moles of sugar is dissolved to form 2 liters of a solution, calculate the molarity of the solution.

a. 1 M solution
b. 1.5 M solution
c. 2 M solution
d. 2.5 M solution

51. Electricity is a general term encompassing a variety of phenomena resulting from the presence and flow of electric charge. Which of the following statements about electricity is/are true?

a. Electrically charged matter is influenced by, and produces, electromagnetic fields.
b. Electric current is a movement or flow of electrically charged particles.
c. Electric potential is a fundamental interaction between the magnetic field and the presence and motion of an electric charge.
d. All of the statements are true.

52. Strong chemical bonds include

a. Dipole - dipole interactions
b. Hydrogen bonding
c. Covalent or ionic bonds
d. None of the above

53. A javelin is thrown into a field at 18 m/s. if the Javelin weighs 1.5 kg, what is the momentum?

a. 1.2 kg x m/s into the field
b. 12 kg x m/s into the field
c. 27 kg x m/s into the field
d. 2.7 kg x m/s into the field

54. Which of these object has greater momentum, a 2 kg truck moving east at 3.5 m/s or a 4.3 kg truck moving south at 1.5 m/s?

a. The first truck at 7 kg x m/s moving east
b. The second truck at 7.45 kg x m/s due south
c. The first truck at 6.45 kg x m/s due east
d. The second truck at 7 kg x m/s due south

55. What is the measure of an experiment's ability to yield the same or compatible results in different clinical experiments or statistical trials?

a. Variability
b. Validity
c. Control measure
d. Reliability

56. Genes control heredity in man and other organisms. This gene is

a. a segment of RNA or DNA.
b. a bead like structure on the chromosomes.
c. a protein molecule.
d. a segment of RNA.

57. One factor that affects rates of reaction is concentration. Which of these statements about concentration is/are correct?

a. A higher concentration of reactants causes more effective collisions per unit time, leading to an increased reaction rate.

b. A lower concentration of reactants causes more effective collisions per unit time, leading to an increased reaction rate.

c. A higher concentration of reactants causes more effective collisions per unit time, leading to a decreased reaction rate.

d. A higher concentration of reactants causes less effective collisions per unit time, leading to an increased reaction rate.

58. Describe each chemical element in the periodic table.

a. Each chemical element has a unique atomic number representing the number of electrons in its nucleus.

b. Each chemical element has a varying atomic number depending on the number of protons in its nucleus.

c. Each chemical element has a unique atomic number representing the number of protons in its nucleus.

d. None of the above.

59. Which of the following statements about nonmetals are true?

a. A nonmetal is a substance that conducts heat and electricity poorly.

b. Most known chemical elements are nonmetals.

c. A nonmetal is brittle or waxy or gaseous.

d. All of the statements are true.

60. The molarity of 5 liters of a salt solution is 0.5 M of salt solution. Calculate the moles of salt in the solution.

a. 2 Moles
b. 2.5 Moles
c. 2.75 Moles
d. 3 Moles

61. A solution with a pH value of less than 7 is

a. Acid solution
b. Base solution
c. Neutral pH solution
d. None of the above

62. What is the distance between adjacent peaks (or adjacent troughs) on a wave?

a. Frequency
b. Wavenumber
c. Wave oscillation
d. Wavelength

63. An object that weighs 500 g is rolling along the road at 3.5 m/s. What is the momentum of the object?

a. 124.9 kg x m/s along road
b. 17. 50 kg x m/s along road
c. 1750 kg x m/s along road
d. 1.75 kg x m/s along road

64. Is a catalyst changed by a reaction?

a. Yes
b. No
c. It may be changed depending on the other chemicals

65. The __________ is the prediction that an observed difference is due to chance alone and not due to a systematic cause; this hypothesis is tested by statistical analysis, and either accepted or rejected.

a. Null hypothesis
b. Hypothesis
c. Control
d. Variable

66. In science, industry, and statistics, the _________ of a measurement system is the degree of closeness of measurements of a quantity to its actual (true) value.

a. Mistake
b. Uncertainty
c. Accuracy
d. Error

67. The horizontal rows of the periodic table are known as

a. Groups
b. Periods
c. Series
d. Columns

68. Which, if any, of these statements about solubility are correct?

a. The solubility of a substance is its concentration in a saturated solution.

b. Substances with solubilities much less than 1 g/100 mL of solvent are usually considered insoluble.

c. A saturated solution is one which does not dissolve any more solute.

d. All of these statements are correct.

69. Describe a valence shell.

a. Is the shell corresponding to the highest value of principal quantum number in the atom.

b. The valence electrons in this shell are on average closer to the nucleus than other electrons.

c. They are rarely directly involved in chemical reaction.

d. None of the above are true.

70. To calculate the Molarity of a solution when the solute is given in grams and the volume of the solution is given in milliliters, you must first

a. Convert grams to moles, but leave the volume of solution in milliliters.

b. Convert volume of solution in milliliters to liters, but leave grams to moles.

c. Convert grams to moles, and convert volume of solution in milliliters to liters.

d. None of the above.

71. What is the atomic number for Hydrogen?

a. 11

b. 2

c. 1

d. 5

72. The vertical columns of the periodic table are known as

a. Series
b. Groups
c. Periods
d. Columns

73. The ____ of a distribution is the difference between the maximum value and the minimum value.

a. Distribution
b. Range
c. Mode
d. Median

74. A cannon ball weighing 35 kg is shot from a cannon towards the east at 220m/s, calculate the momentum of the cannon ball.

a. 7500 kg m/s east
b. 7700 kg m/s east
c. 8000 kg m/s east
d. 8500 kg m/s east

75. Which, if any, of the following statements describing acids are correct?

a. An acid is a compound containing detachable hydrogen ions.
b. An acid is a compound that can accept a pair of electrons from a base.
c. A and B are correct
d. None of the above

Answer Key

1. A

Choice B is incorrect; the author did not express their opinion on the subject matter. Choice C is incorrect, the author was not trying to prove a point, nor is the author trying to persuade.

2. C

Choice C is correct; historians believe it was brutal and bloody. Choice A is incorrect; there is no consensus that the Crusades achieved great things. Choice B is incorrect; it did not stabilize the Holy Lands. Choice D is incorrect, some historians do believe this was the purpose but not all historians.

3. D

The feudal system led to infighting. Choice A is incorrect, it had the opposite effect. Choice B is incorrect, though this is a good answer, it is not the best answer. The Church asked for volunteers not the Feudal Lords. Choice C is incorrect, it did have an effect on the Crusades.

4. A

Saracen was a generic term for Muslims widely used in Europe during the later medieval era.

5. B

This warranty does not cover a product that you have tried to fix yourself. From paragraph two, "This limited warranty does not cover … any unauthorized disassembly, repair, or modification. "

6. C

ABC Electric could either replace or repair the fan, provided the other conditions are met. ABC Electric has the option to repair or replace.

7. B

The warranty does not cover a stove damaged in a flood. From the passage, "This limited warranty does not cover any damage to the product from improper installation, accident, abuse, misuse, natural disaster, insufficient or excessive electrical supply, abnormal mechanical or environmental conditions."

A flood is an "abnormal environmental condition," and a natural disaster, so it is not covered.

8. A

A missing part is an example of defective workmanship. This is an error made in the manufacturing process. A defective part is not considered workmanship.

9. D

This question tests the reader's summarization skills. The other choices A, B, and C focus on portions of the second paragraph that are too narrow and do not relate to the specific portion of text in question. The complexity of the sentence may mislead students into selecting one of these answers, but rearranging or restating the sentence will lead the reader to the correct answer. In addition, choice A makes an assumption that may or may not be true about the intentions of the company, choice B focuses on one product rather than the idea of the products, and choice C makes an assumption about women that may or may not be true and is not supported by the text.

10. B

This question tests reader's attention to detail. If a reader selects A, he or she may have picked up on the use of the word "debate" and assumed, very logically, that the two are at odds because they are fighting; however, this is simply not supported in the text. Choice C also uses very specific quotes from the text, but it rearranges and gives them false meaning. The artists want to elevate their creations above the creations of other artists, thereby showing that they are "creative" and "innovative." Similarly, choice D takes phrases straight from the text and rearranges and confuses them. The artists are described as wanting to be "creative, innovative, individual people," not the women.

11. A

This question tests reader's vocabulary and summarization skills. This phrase, used by the author, may seem flippant and dismissive if readers focus on the word "whatever" and misinterpret it as a popular, colloquial term. In this way, choices B and C may mislead the reader to selecting one of them by including the terms "unimportant" and "stupid," respectively. Choice D is a similar misreading, but doesn't make sense when the phrase is at the beginning of the passage and the entire passage is on media messages. Choice A is literally and contextually appropriate, and the reader can understand that the author would like to keep the introduction focused on the topic the passage is going to discuss.

12. A

This question tests a reader's inference skills. The extreme use of the word "all" in choice B suggests that every single advertising company are working to be approachable, and while this is not only unlikely, the text specifically states that "more" companies have done this, signifying that they have not all participated, even if it's a possibility that they may some day. The use of the limiting word "only" in choice C lends that answer similar problems; women are still buying from companies who do not care about this message, or those companies would not be in business, and the passage specifies that "many" women are worried about media messages, but not all. Readers may find choice D logical, especially if they are looking to make an inference, and while this may be a possibility, the passage does not suggest or discuss this happening. Choice A is correct based on specifically because of the relation between "still working" in the answer and "will hopefully" and the extensive discussion on companies struggles, which come only with progress, in the text.

13. C

This question tests the reader's summarization skills. The entire passage is leading up to the idea that the president of the US may not have had grounds to assert his Fourteen Points when other countries had lost so much. Choice A is pretty directly inferred by the text, but it does not adequately summarize what the entire passage is trying to communicate. Choice B may also be inferred by the passage when it says that the war is "imminent," but it does not represent the entire message, either. The passage does seem to be in praise of FDR, or at least in respect of him, but it does not in any way claim that he is the smartest president, nor does this represent the many other points included. Choice C is then the obvious answer, and most directly relates to the closing sentences which it rewords.

14. C

This question tests the reader's attention to detail. The passage does state that choices A and B are true, and while those statements are in proximity to the explanation for why the war started, they are not the reason given. Choice D is a mix up of words used in the passage, which says that the largest powers were in play but not that this fact somehow started the war. The passage does make a direct statement that a domino effect started the war, supporting choice C as the correct answer.

15. A

This question tests the reader's understanding of functions in writing. Throughout the passage, it states that leaders of other nations were hesitant to accept generous or peaceful terms because of the grievances of the war, and the great loss of life was chief among these. While the passage does touch on the devastation of deadly weapons (B), the use of this raw, emotional fact serves a much larger purpose, and the focus of the passage is not the weapons. While readers may indeed consider who lost the most soldiers (C) when, so many countries were involved and the inequalities of loss are mentioned in the passage, there is no discussion of this in the passage. Choice D is related to A, but choice A is more direct and relates more to the passage.

16. B

This question tests the reader's vocabulary skills. Choice A may seem appealing to readers because it is phonetically similar to "catalysed," but the two are not related in any other way. Choice C makes sense in context, but if plugged in to the sentence creates a redundancy that doesn't make sense. Choice D does also not make sense contextually, even if the reader may consider that funds were needed to create more weaponry, especially if it was advanced.

17. A

Victoria is about 5 miles from Burnaby.

18. B
The Village Hall is about 5 miles from Victoria.

19. A
The correct order of ingredients is brown sugar, baking soda and chocolate chips.

20. B
Sturdy: strong, solid in structure or person. In context, Stir in chocolate chips by hand with a *sturdy* wooden spoon.

21. A
Disperse: to scatter in different directions or break up. In context, Stir until the chocolate chips and nuts are evenly *dispersed.*

22. B
You can stop stirring the nuts when they are evenly distributed. From the passage, "Stir until the chocolate chips and nuts are evenly dispersed."

23. B
This question tests the reader's summarization skills. Choice A is a very broad statement that may or may not be true, and seems to be in context, but has nothing to do with the passage. The author does mention that the statue was probably used on a temple dedicated to the Greek gods (D), but in no way discusses or argues for the gods' attitude toward or claim on these temples or its faucets. Nike does indeed lead the gods into a war (the Titan war), as choice C suggests, but this is not mentioned by the passage and students who know this may be drawn to this answer but have not done a close enough analysis of the text that is actually in the passage. Choice B is appropriately expository, and connects the titular emphasis to the idea that the Greek gods are very important to Greek culture.

24. C
This question tests the reader's summarization skills. The test for question choice C is pulled straight from the paragraph, but is not word-for-word, so it may seem too obvious to be the right answer. The passage does talk about Nike being the goddess of war, as choice A states, but the

third paragraph only touches on it and it is an inference that soldiers destroyed the statue, when this question is asking specifically for what the third paragraph actually stated. Choice B is also straight from the text, with a minor but key change: the inclusion of the words "all" and "never" are too limiting and the passage does not suggest that these limits exist. If a reader selects choice D, they are also making an inference that is misguided for this type of question. The paragraph does state that the arms and head are "lost" but does not suggest who lost them.

25. A

This question tests the reader's ability to recognize function in writing. Choice B can be eliminated based on the purpose of the passage, which is expository and not persuasive. The author may or may not feel this way, but the passage does not show evidence of being argumentative for that purpose. Choices C and D are both details found in the text, but neither of them encompasses the entire message of the passage, which has an overall message of learning about culture from art and making guesses about how the two are related, as suggested by choice A.

26. D

This question tests the reader's ability to understand function within writing. Most of the possible selections are very general statements which may or may not be true. It probably is a student who is taking the test on which this question is featured (A), but the author makes no address to the test taker and is not talking to the audience in terms of the test. Likewise, it may also be true students read more than adults (C), mandated by schools and grades, but the focus on the verb "read" in the first sentence is too narrow and misses the larger purpose of the passage; the same could be said for selection B. While all the statements could be true, choice D is the most germane, and infers the purpose of the passage without making assumptions that could be incorrect.

27. B

The time limit for radar detectors is 14 days. Since you made the purchase 15 days ago, you do not qualify for the guarantee.

28. B

Since you made the purchase 10 days ago, you are covered by the guarantee. Since it is an advertised price at a different store, ABC Electric will "beat" the price by 10% of the difference, which is,

500 – 400 = 100 – difference in price

100 X 10% = $10 – 10% of the difference

The advertised lower price is $400. ABC will beat this price by 10% so they will refund $100 + 10 = $110.

29. C

The purpose of this passage is to persuade.

30. B

The correct answer can be found in the fourth sentence of the first paragraph.

Choice A is incorrect because repenting begins the day AFTER Mardi Gras. Choice C is incorrect because you can celebrate Mardi Gras without being a member of a Krewe.

Choice D is incorrect because exploration does not play any role in a modern Mardi Gras celebration.

31. A

The second sentence is the last paragraph states that Krewes are led by the Kings and Queens. Therefore, you must have to be part of a Krewe to be its King or its Queen.

Choice B is incorrect because it never states in the passage that only people from France can be Kings and Queen of Mardi Gras

Choice C is incorrect because the passage says nothing about having to speak French.

Choice D is incorrect because the passage does state that the Kings and Queens throw doubloons, which is fake money.

32. C

The first sentences of BOTH the 2nd and 3rd paragraphs

mention that French explorers started this tradition in New Orleans.
Choices A, B and D are incorrect because they are names of cities or countries listed in the 2nd paragraph.

33. B
In the final paragraph, the word spectator is used to describe people who are watching the parade and catching cups, beads and doubloons.

Choices A and C are incorrect because we know the people who participate are part of Krewes. People who work the floats and parades are also part of Krewes

Choice D is incorrect because the passage makes no mention of people who do not celebrate Mardi Gras.

Verbal Ability Part II – Vocabulary

34. B
Heinous: adj. shocking, terrible or wicked.

35. A
Harbinger: n. a person of thing that tells or announces the coming of someone or something

36. B
Judicious: Having, or characterized by, good judgment or sound thinking.

37. B
Ethanol: n. a colorless volatile flammable liquid C2H6O.

38. A
Respiratory: adj. Of, relating to, or affecting respiration or the organs of respiration.

39. B
Inherent: Naturally a part or consequence of something.

40. A
Vapid: adj. tasteless or bland.
41. C
Waif: n. homeless child or stray.

42. D
Homologous: adj. similar or identical.

43. B
Obsolete: adj. no longer in use; gone into disuse; disused or neglected.

44. A
Rankle: v. To cause irritation or deep bitterness.

45. D
Reusable

46. C
Torpid: adj. Lazy, lethargic or apathetic.

47. A
Gregarious: adj. Describing one who enjoys being in crowds and socializing.

48. B
Mutation: n. a change or alteration.
49. C
Lithe: adj. flexible or pliant.

50. A
Resent: v. to express displeasure or indignation.

51. A
Immaterial: adj. irrelevant not having substance or matter.

52. A
Impeccable: adj. perfect, no faults or errors.

53. B
Pudgy: adj. fat, plump or overweight.

54. C
Alloy: v. Mix or combine; often used of metals.

55. B
Combustible: adj. Able to catch fire and burn easily.

56. C
Salient: adj. Worthy of note; pertinent or relevant.

57. B
Ulterior: adj. beyond what is obvious or evident.

58. D
Junta: n. ruling council of a military government.

59. C
Laggard: n. someone who takes more time than necessary.

60. B
Languid: adj. lacking enthusiasm, strength or energy.

Section II – Math

1. D
$x^2 + 4x = 5$, $x^2 + 4x - 5 = 0$, $x^2 + 5x - x - 5 = 0$, factoring $x(x + 5) - 1(x + 5) = 0$, $(x + 5)(x-1)=0$. $x + 5 = 0$ or $x - 1 = 0$, $x = 0 - 5$ or $x = 0 + 1$, $x = -5$ or $x = 1$, either b or c.

2. C
Open parenthesis: $2a + 2b = 4ab$, divide both sides by 2 = $a + b = 2ab$ or $a + b = ab + ab$, therefore $a = ab$ and $b = ab$, therefore $a = b$.

3. B
Let the XY represent the initial number, X + Y = 12, YX = XY+ 36, Only b = 48 satisfies both equations above from the given choices.

4. B

Number of absent students = 83 – 72 = 11

Percentage of absent students is found by proportioning the number of absent students to the total number of students in the class = (11 * 100)/83 = 13.25

Checking the answers, we round 13.25 to the nearest whole number: 13%

5. B
Let the father's age=Y, and Kate's age=X, therefore Y=32+X, in 5yrs y=5x,substituting for Y will be 5x = 32+X, 5x – x = 32, 4X=32,X= 32/8, x = 8, Kate will be 8 in 5 yrs time, so Kate's present age = 8 - 5 = 3.

6. A
This is a simple direct proportion problem:

If Lynn can type 1 page in p minutes,

she can type x pages in 5 minutes

Cross multiply: x * p = 5 * 1

Then, x = 5/p

7. A
First add all the numbers 2.5 + 9.5 + 4.5 + 1.25 + 7.05 + 20.8 = 45.6. Then divide by 6 (the number of data provided) = 45.6/6 = 7.6

8. A
This is an inverse ration problem.

1/x = 1/a + 1/b where a is the time Sally can paint a house, b is the time John can paint a house, x is the time Sally and John can together paint a house.

So,

1/x = 1/4 + 1/6 ... We use the least common multiple in the denominator that is 24:

1/x = 6/24 + 4/24

$1/x = 10/24$

$x = 24/10$

$x = 2.4$ hours.

In other words; 2 hours + 0.4 hours = 2 hours + 0.4 * 60 minutes

= 2 hours 24 minutes

9. B

First convert 350g to kg = 350/1000 = 0.35kg. Momentum of bullet = 0.35 x 250 = 87.5 kg x m/s towards target

10. A

To solve the equation, we need the equation in the form $ax^2 + bx + c = 0$.

$x^2 - 9x + 14 = 0$ is already in this form.

The quadratic formula to find the roots of a quadratic equation is:

$x_{1,2} = (-b \pm \sqrt{\Delta}) / 2a$ where $\Delta = b^2 - 4ac$ and is called the discriminant of the quadratic equation.

In our question, the equation is $x^2 - 9x + 14 = 0$. By remembering the form $ax^2 + bx + c = 0$:

$a = 1, b = -9, c = 14$

So, we can find the discriminant first, and then the roots of the equation:

$\Delta = b^2 - 4ac = (-9)^2 - 4 \cdot 1 \cdot 14 = 81 - 56 = 25$

$x_{1,2} = (-b \pm \sqrt{\Delta}) / 2a = (-(-9) \pm \sqrt{25}) / 2 = (9 \pm 5) / 2$

This means that the roots are,

$x_1 = (9 - 5) / 2 = 2$ and $x_2 = (9 + 5) / 2 = 7$

11. D

The cost of the dishwasher = $450

15% discount amount = (450 * 15)/100 = $67.5

The discounted price = 450 – 67.5 = $382.5

20% additional discount amount on lowest price = (382.5 * 20)/100 = $76.5

So, the final discounted price = 382.5 - 76.5 = $306.00

12. D
Original price = x,
80/100 = 12590/X,
80X = 1259000,
X = 15737.50.

13. C
Total hay = 214 kg,
The goat eats at a rate of 214/60 days = 3.6 kg per day.
The Cow eats at a rate of 214/15 = 14.3 kg per day,
Together they eat 3.6 + 14.3 = 17.9 per day.
At a rate of 17.9 kg per day, they will consume 214 kg in 214/17.9 = 11.96 or 12 days approximately.

14. C
125/100 = 1.25

15 B
The smallest prime number that can divide 125 is 5. 125/5 = 25. 25/5 =5. Prime factors of 125 = 5 x 5 x5

16. D
40/100 = 30/X = 40X = 30 * 100 = 3000/40 = 75

17. A
Momentum of first object = 2 x 3.5 = 7; momentum of second truck = 4.3 x 1.5 = 6.45. First truck has more momentum at 7 kg x m/s moving east

18. B
12.5/100 = 50/X = 12.5X = 50 * 100 = 5000/12.5 = 400

19. C
24/56 = 3/7 (divide numerator and denominator by 8)

20. D
The smallest prime number to divide 132 is 2. 132/2 = 66. 66/2 = 33. 33/3 = 11. 11 cannot be divided further by a prime number other than 11. The prime numbers of 132 = 2 x 2 x 3 x 11

21. C
Converting percent to decimal – divide percent by 100 and remove the % sign. 87% = 87/100 = .87

22. A
60 has the same relation to X as 75 to 100 – so
60/X = 75/100
6000 = 75X
X = 80

23. B
First arrange the numbers in a numerical sequence – 43, 45, 50, 65, 66, 69, 73, 75, 77, 80, 86, 90, 91. Next find the middle number. The median = 73

24. C
4.7 + .9 + .01 = 5.61

25. A
.87 - .48 = .39

26. A
Step 1: Set up the formula to calculate the dose to be given in mg as per weight of the child:-
Dose ordered X Weight in Kg = Dose to be given
Step 2: 100 mg X 23 kg = 2300 mg
(Convert 50 lb to Kg, 1 lb = 0.4536 kg, hence 50 lb = 50 X 0.4536 = 22.68 kg approx. 23 kg)
2300 mg/230 mg X 1 tablet/1 = 2300/230 = 10 tablets

27. D

Simply find the most recurring number. All the numbers in the series appeared only once. The answer is No Mode

28. C

4 x 4 x 4 = 64

29. D

5 ml/15 ml kX 1 tsp/1 = 5/15 = 0.3 tsp

30. B

To solve the equation, first we need to arrange it to appear in the form $ax^2 + bx + c = 0$ by removing the denominator:

$x - 31/x = 0$ … First, we enlarge the equation by x:

$x \cdot x - 31 \cdot x/x = 0$

$x^2 - 31 = 0$

The quadratic formula to find the roots of a quadratic equation is:

$x_{1,2} = (-b \pm \sqrt{\Delta}) / 2a$ where $\Delta = b^2 - 4ac$ and is called the discriminant of the quadratic equation.

In our question, the equation is $x^2 - 31 = 0$. By remembering the form $ax^2 + bx + c = 0$:

$a = 1, b = 0, c = -31$

So, we can find the discriminant first, and then the roots of the equation:

$\Delta = b^2 - 4ac = 0^2 - 4 \cdot 1 \cdot (-31) = 124$

$x_{1,2} = (-b \pm \sqrt{\Delta}) / 2a = (\pm\sqrt{124}) / 2 = (\pm\sqrt{4 \cdot 31}) / 2 = (\pm 2\sqrt{31}) / 2$ … Simplifying by 2:

$x_{1,2} = \pm\sqrt{31}$ … This means that the roots are $\sqrt{31}$ and $-\sqrt{31}$.

31. A

At 100% efficiency 1 machine produces 1450/10 = 145 m of cloth.

At 95% efficiency, 4 machines produce (4 * 145 * 95)/100 = 551 m of cloth.

At 90% efficiency, 6 machines produce (6 * 145 * 90)/100 = 783 m of cloth.

Total cloth produced by all 10 machines = 551 + 783 = 1334 m

Since the information provided and the question are based on 8 hours, we did not need to use time to reach the answer.

32. D
Perimeter of triangle ABC is asked.
Perimeter of a triangle = sum of the three sides.

Here, Perimeter of ΔABC = |AC| + |CB| + |AB|.

Since the triangle is located in the middle of two adjacent and identical rectangles, we find the side lengths using these rectangles:

|AB| = 6 + 6 = 12 cm

|CB| = 8.5 cm

|AC| = |CB| = 8.5 cm

Perimeter = |AC| + |CB| + |AB| = 8.5 + 8.5 + 12 = 29 cm

33. A
10 x 10 x 100 x 100 = 1000^x, =100 x 10,000 = 1000^x, = 1,000,000 = 1000^x = x =2

34. B
a + b + c + d = ?
The sum of angles around a point is 360°
a + b + c + d = 360°

35. C
Simply find the most recurring number. The most occurring numbers in the series is 2 and 6

36. A
The scientific notation is in the positive so we shift the decimal 6 places to the right. Thus it is 5,630,000

37. D
There are 1000 mg in a gram. 30/1000 = 0.03 grams. To

divide by 1000, move the decimal 3 places to the left. =

38. A

The shape is made of a square and a semi circle. Calculate the perimeter of each and add.

Perimeter = 3 sides of the square + ½ circumference of the circle.

= (3 x 5) + ½(5 π)

= 15 + 2.5 π

Perimeter = 17.5 π cm

39. A

There are 10 mm in a cm. 0.101/10 = .0101. To divide by 10, move the decimal 1 place to the left.

40. A

$2x^2 - 3x = 0$ ... we see that both of the terms contain x; so we can take it out as a factor:

$x(2x - 3) = 0$ ... two terms are multiplied and the result is zero. This means that either of the terms or both of the terms can be equal to zero:

x = 0 ... this is one of the solutions

2x - 3 = 0 → 2x = 3 → x = 3/2 → x = 1.5 ... this is the second solution.

So, the solutions are 0 and 1.5.

41. B

The formula of the volume of cylinder is the base area multiplied by the height. As the formula:

Volume of a cylinder = $\pi r^2 h$. Where π is 3.142, r is radius of the cross sectional area, and h is the height.

We know that the diameter is 5 meters, so the radius is 5/2 = 2.5 meters.

The volume is: V = 3.142 * 2.52 * 12 = 235.65 m^3.

42. A

The decimal point moves 2 spaces to the left to be placed after 4, which is the first non-zero number. 4.5×10^{-2} The exponent is negation since the decimal moved left.

43. D

The relation is the same figure rotated.

44. D

The shaded area is divided in half in the second figure.

45. D

The relation is the same figure rotated to the right.

46. B

The relation is the number of dots is one-half the number of sides.

47. D

First, we need to search for a constant common factor in each of the terms. If there is any, we need to take it out of the equation and write it as a coefficient in front:
$9x^2 - 6x + 12 = 3(3x^2 - 2x + 4)$

We cannot go further from this point, so this is the factored form of the polynomial

48. C

389 + 454 = 843

49. C

9,177 + 7,204 = 16,381

50. D

2,199 + 5,832 = 8,031

Section III – Science

1. A

The formula for acceleration = A = $(V_f - V_0)/t$
so A = (0 - 12)/60 sec = -0.2 m/sec^2

2. A

The Law of Multiple Proportions states that when two elements combine to form more than one compound, the weights of one element that combine with a fixed weight of the other are in a ratio of small whole numbers.

3. D

All of the above are true. Electrons play an essential role in electricity, magnetism, and thermal conductivity.

4. D

An idea concerning a phenomena and possible explanations for that phenomena is an hypothesis.

5. D

All of the above. Chromosomes are

a. Structures in a cell nucleus that carry genetic material.

b. Consist of thousands of DNA strands.

c. Total 46 in a normal human cell.

6. D

All of the statements about bases are true.

a. A compound that reacts with an acid to form a salt.

b. A molecule or ion that captures hydrogen ions.

c. A molecule or ion that donates an electron pair to form a chemical bond.

7. D

The circulatory system disease that is one of the most frequent causes of death in North America is heart disease.

8. B

Speed = (total distance traveled)/(total time taken)
X = 1000m/20 minutes
X = 50 meters

9. A

A chemical compound is a chemical substance comprising atoms from two or more elements in a specific ration as expressed in the chemical formula i.e., H2O

10. C

The plasma membrane or cell membrane protects the cell from outside forces. It consists of the lipid bilayer with embedded proteins

11. C

Protein biosynthesis is defines as, ribosomes synthesizing proteins in the endoplasmic reticulum. This process, also known as protein biosynthesis, is a process within the cell by which the substrates convert to products of higher complexity.

12. A

Cell fractionation. Fractionation is important because it purifies the cell and its parts.

13. A

The Strong Nuclear Force is an attractive force that binds protons and neutrons and maintains the structure of the nucleus, and the Weak Nuclear Force is responsible for the radioactive beta decay and other subatomic reactions.

14. B

Force = Mass times Acceleration Measured in Newtons.
1000 = 500 x A
A = 1000/500 = 2 m/s^2

15. D

Qualitative research deals with the quality, type or components of a group, substance, or mixture.

16. B

When a measurement is recorded, it includes the significant figures, which are all the digits that are certain plus one uncertain digit.

17. B

The equation $E = mc^2$ is based on the Law of Conservation of Mass and Energy, and states that Energy equals Mass times the Velocity of light ^{2}.

18. A

A pH indicator measures hydrogen ions in a solution and show pH on a color scale.

19. B

Acids turns blue litmus paper red, base turns red litmus paper blue.

20. A

Covalent bonds involve a complete sharing of electrons and occurs most commonly between atoms that have partially filled outer shells or energy levels.

21. C

A base is any substance that can accept a hydrogen ion and can react with fats to form soap.

22. A

Water boils at approximately 100 °C (212 °F) at standard atmospheric pressure.

23. D

The dominant gene controls the expression of a trait.

24. D

Wavefunction is a mathematical function that gives the amplitude of a wave as a function of position (and sometimes, as a function of time and/or electron spin).

25. B

The vacuum of space is an environment where bacteria do not commonly exit. The nature of outer space, including intense cold and lack of oxygen, makes it difficult for even most bacteria to grow.

26. B

Plants and animals are kingdoms. There are six recognized kingdoms: Animalia, Plantae, Protista, Fungi, Bacteria, and Archaea.

27. C

Force = Mass times Acceleration Measured in Newtons.
F = 2000 kg X 3 m/sec^2 = 6000 N

28. C

A catalyst is a chemical involved in, but not changed by, a chemical reaction by which chemical bonds are weakened and reactions accelerated.

29. C

Organisms grouped into the **Protista** Kingdom include all unicellular organisms lacking a definite cellular arrangement such as **bacteria** and **algae.**

30. C

All of these statements are true.

> A metal is a substance that conducts heat and electricity.
>
> A metal is shiny and reflects many colors of light, and can be hammered into sheets or drawn into wire.
>
> About 80% of the known chemical elements are metals.

31. C

The reaction of elements with low electronegativity(almost empty outer shells) with elements with high electronegativity (mostly full outer shells) gives rise to Ionic bonds.

32. D

AIDS (or Acquired Immune Deficiency Syndrome) is carried by a virus, not bacteria.

33. A

A collection of similar or like living entities. Class has the same meaning in biology as rank. Common classes or ranks include species, order, and phylum.

34. D

All of these statements are true.

> a. Prokaryotic cells include such organisms as E. coli and Streptococcus.
>
> b. Prokaryotic cells lack internal membranes and organelles.
>
> c. Prokaryotic cells break down food using cellular respiration and fermentation.

35. B

Force = Mass times Acceleration Measured in Newtons.
1000 = 500 x A
A = 1000/500 = 2 m/s^2

36. B

The process of converting observed phenomena into data is called measurement.

37. A

The Law of Multiple Proportions states that when two elements combine to form more than one compound, the weights of one element that combine with a fixed weight of the other are in a ratio of small whole numbers.

38. A

Morphology is the field that studies the relationship between structures in living organisms.

39. A

The mass number of an atom is the total number of particles (protons and neutrons) that make it up.

40. A

All of the statements are true.

a. Mechanical energy is the energy that is possessed by an object due to its motion or due to its position.

b. Mechanical energy can be either kinetic energy (energy of motion) or potential energy (stored energy of position).

c. Objects have mechanical energy if they are in motion

41. D

In Eukaryotic cells, the cell cycle is the cycle of events involving cell division, including mitosis, cytokinesis, and interphase.

42. B

The atomic number of an element equals the number of protons in an atomic nucleus, and, along with the element symbol is one of two alternate ways to label an element.

43. A

pH is a measure of effective concentration of hydrogen ions in a solution, and is approximately related to the molarity of H+ by pH = - log [H+]

44. B

Ribonucleic acid (RNA) is a chain of nucleotides that plays an important role in the creation of new proteins.

45. C

Force = Mass times Acceleration Measured in Newtons.
F = 200 X 5 = 1000 N

46. D

The Law of Definite Proportions states that every chemical compound contains fixed and constant proportions (by weight) of its constituent elements.

47. B

Four factors that affect rates of reaction are: Temperature, particle size, concentration, and the presence of a catalyst.

48. C

Spherical bacteria are Cocci. Along with bacilli, this is one of the two major structures for bacteria.

49. A

A practical test designed with the intention that its results will be relevant to a particular theory or set of theories is an experiment.

50. B

The formula for calculating molarity when the moles of the solute and liters of the solution are given is = moles of solute/ liters of solution.
Moles of Solute = 3 moles of sugar
Solution liters = 3 liters
Molarity of solution = ?

Therefore: molarity of the solution = 3 moles of solvent/ 2 liters of solution = 1.5 M solution.

51. D

All of the statements are true.

a. Electrically charged matter is influenced by, and produces, electromagnetic fields.

b. Electric current is a movement or flow of electrically charged particles.

c. Electric potential is a fundamental interaction between the magnetic field and the presence and motion of an electric charge.

52. C
Covalent or ionic bonds are considered "strong bonds."

53. C
P = 1.5 x 18 = 27 kg x m/s into the field.

54. A
Momentum of first object = 2 x 3.5 = 7; momentum of second truck = 4.3 x 1.5 = 6.45. First truck has more momentum at 7 kg x m/s moving east.

55. D
Reliability refers to the measure of an experiment's ability to yield the same or compatible results in different clinical experiments or statistical trials.

56. A
Genes are made from a long molecule called DNA, which is copied and inherited across generations. DNA is made of simple units that line up in a particular order within this large molecule. The order of these units carries genetic information, similar to how the order of letters on a page carries information. The language used by DNA is called the genetic code, which lets organisms read the information in the genes. This information is the instructions for constructing and operating a living organism.

57. A
A higher concentration of reactants causes more effective collisions per unit time, leading to an increased reaction rate.

58. C
Each chemical element has a unique atomic number representing the number of protons in its nucleus.

59. D

All of these statements are about non-metals are true.

a. A nonmetal is a substance that conducts heat and electricity poorly.

b. Most known chemical elements are nonmetals.

c. A nonmetal is brittle or waxy or gaseous.

60. B

Moles of solute = ? or X
Solutions liters = 5 liters
Molarity of solution = 0.5 M
Therefore: X moles/5 liters of solution = 0.5 or X/5 = 0.5
So X = 5/0.5
X = 2.5
Mole of salt in the solution is 2.5 moles

61. A

A solution with a pH value of less than 7 is acid. A pH value of 7 is neutral.

62. D

Wavelength is defined as the distance between adjacent peaks (or adjacent troughs) on a wave.

Note: Varying the wavelength of light changes its color; varying the wavelength of sound changes its pitch.

63. D

First convert 500 g to kg = 500/1000 = 0.5 kg, momentum = 0.5 x 3.5 = 1.75 kg x m/s along the road.

64. B

A catalyst is never changed in a chemical reaction.

65. A

The prediction that an observed difference is due to chance alone and not due to a systematic cause; this hypothesis is tested by statistical analysis, and accepted or rejected is the **null hypothesis**.

66. C

In science and engineering, the **accuracy** of a measurement system is the degree of closeness of measurements of a quantity to its actual (true) value.

67. B

The horizontal rows from right to left of the periodic table are known as periods and elements on a row share the same number of electron shells.

68. D

All of the statements about solubility are correct.

a. The solubility of a substance is its concentration in a saturated solution.

b. Substances with solubilities much less than 1 g/100 mL of solvent are usually considered insoluble.

c. A saturated solution is one which does not dissolve any more solute.

69. A

A valence shell is the shell corresponding to the highest value of principal quantum number in the atom.

70. C

To calculate the Molarity of a solution when the solute is given in grams and the volume of the solution is given in milliliters, you must first **convert grams to moles, and convert volume of solution in milliliters to liters.**

71. C

Hydrogen is the first element listed on the periodic table. The atomic number for hydrogen is 1.

72. B

Vertical columns on the periodic table are called groups. There are 18 groups on the table. Elements in the same group have the same number of electrons on their outermost shell.

73. B

The **range** of a distribution is the difference between the maximum value and the minimum value.

74. B

Formula - P= kg x m/s
= 35kg x 220 m/s
= 7700 kg x m/s east

75. C

A and B are correct.
An acid is a compound containing detachable hydrogen ions.
An acid is a compound that can accept a pair of electrons from a base.

PRACTICE TESTS 3 AND 4

Join us online for over 340 more practice questions (completely FREE) including a timed PAX Test to get ready for the real thing!

Go to https://courses.test-preparation.ca/course?courseid=pax3-4 and use coupon PAX34

CONCLUSION

CONGRATULATIONS! You have made it this far because you have applied yourself diligently to practicing for the exam and no doubt improved your potential score considerably! Getting into a good school is a huge step in a journey that might be challenging at times but will be many times more rewarding and fulfilling. That is why being prepared is so important.

Study then Practice and then Succeed!

Good Luck!

Register for Free Updates and More Practice Test Questions

Register your purchase at https://www.test-preparation.ca/register/ for fast and convenient access to updates, free test tips and more

https://www.facebook.com/CompleteTestPreparation/

https://www.youtube.com/user/MrTestPreparation

https://www.instagram.com/test.preparation/

www.ingramcontent.com/pod-product-compliance
Lightning Source LLC
LaVergne TN
LVHW050641100826
845148LV00011B/1939